# 24 FOOTPA
# AROUND S'

*With notes on Po*

## PUBLISHED BY
# ST ALBANS & DISTRICT
# FOOTPATHS SOCIETY

(Reg. Charity No. 1039715)

First Edition 1988
Second Edition 1990; Reprinted 1991
Third Edition 1993; Reprinted 1997
Fourth Edition 2000
Fifth Edition 2004
Sixth Edition 2010
Seventh Edition 2019; Reprinted 2020

# INTRODUCTION

This book is published by the St Albans & District Footpaths Society (the Society). The Society, now a registered charity, started life in 1967, and a booklet describing walks entitled *"Footpath Walks around St Albans"* was published in 1971. In 1978 this was followed by leaflets describing walks, which were revised in 1982. *"24 Footpath Walks around St Albans"*, known colloquially as "the green book", was first published in 1988. This is the seventh edition, with total sales of previous editions exceeding 21,000. The Society has also produced a book covering walks further afield, entitled *"24 Footpath Walks in Hertfordshire"*, known as "the brown book".

Text for each walk describes a circular walk with Item numbers in the text corresponding to numbers on each associated map. This edition has three new routes (Walks 16, 17, and 19), three with significant changes (Walks 15, 21, and 23), and four with revised starting places (Walks 5, 9, 14, and 24). A number of walks have one or more alternatives, indicated in Red or Blue. Points of Interest are now indicated by *[POI]* in the text where they apply. The number refers to the list starting on page 60.

Text and maps for each walk have been checked and, where necessary, changes made to the previous edition.

Details for each walk are accurate at the time of going to press, but changes can occur quickly and landmarks disappear. The Society cannot accept responsibility for any changes that may occur over time, nor for any accident sustained by walkers whilst using this book.

If problems are experienced which relate to the **book**, please email the Society at: **stalbansfootpaths@gmail.com** stating Walk and Item number(s), together with the Grid Reference of each location.

For problems experienced with the **state** of the rights of way (such as obstructions, overgrowth, or missing waymarks), please notify the Society as above, or contact Hertfordshire County Council (HCC) Countryside Rights of Way (CROW) team at: **www.hertfordshire.gov.uk/services/recycling-waste-and-environment/ countryside-access/rights of way/rights of way.aspx**

# ACKNOWLEDGEMENTS

Thanks go to the many Society members involved in this latest edition: walking the routes, identifying changes in text and map alike, and cross-checking. Thanks also go to Mike Marriott, John Leng, Peter Lawrence, Quentin Keeling and Jane Kerr who have overseen the final preparation of this edition, and to John Howes who has redrawn the maps and sketches. For many years Bill Frost was editor-in-chief of previous editions of this book.

Thanks also go to Jane Kerr who has been invaluable in maintaining the high sales and wide distribution of our books.

For several years, proceeds from the sale of our books has enabled the Society to help finance a range of relevant projects in the district.

# ABOUT THE SOCIETY

The Society was inaugurated in 1967 by a small group of people concerned about the state of paths in our district. Our first Chairman was H L (Dick) Knapp, for 15 years. Our primary objective is to preserve, protect, and enhance footpaths and public rights of way. Since 1967, many Society members (including our parish footpath representatives) have regularly checked all the District's rights of way for obstructions, overgrowth, missing waymarks, and other problems. We report these to HCC CROW. The Society also has a work group who help keep paths clear, coordinating with HCC CROW, and guided by the Acts on page 4.

As well as producing walks books and checking paths, we organise walks on Thursday mornings (usually two each week), and most Sundays. Walkers, both past and present, meet monthly in St Albans for coffee; we also hold occasional social events each year, such as a summer picnic, garden party and a Christmas or New Year lunch.

If you are interested in joining the Society, or would like more information, email us at: **stalbansfootpaths@gmail.com**
or visit our website at : **http://www.stalbansfootpaths.org**

We wish all readers happy and enjoyable walking.

# COUNTRYSIDE & RIGHTS OF WAY ACT (2000)

Relevant extracts from this Act are given below. A link to the full Act is:
**http://www.legislation.gov.uk/ukpga/2000/37/contents**

The following should not be ploughed or disturbed if they can be conveniently be avoided:

- Cross-field footpaths and bridleways
- Footpaths or bridleways at the edge of the field

The occupier may plough or disturb the surface of a footpath which crosses a field. But it must then be made sure that:

- The surface is made good, so that it is reasonably convenient to use
- The line is apparent on the ground

This must be done within 14 days of the first disturbance for that crop.

Crops, other than grass, must not be allowed to grow on or overhang the footpath or bridleway, so as to inconvenience the public or prevent the line of the right of way from being apparent on the ground.

"Minimum Width" (if not explicitly recorded) means:

- For a footpath, 1m across a field, 1.5m on a field edge
- For a bridleway, 2m across a field, 3m on a field edge
- Other rights of way, 3m across a field, 5m at a field edge

# COUNTRYSIDE CODE (2016)

A link to this Code is:
**www.gov.uk/government/publications/the-countryside-code**

**Respect** other people

- Consider the local community and other people enjoying the outdoors
- Leave gates and property as you find them, and follow paths unless wider access is available

**Protect** the natural environment

- Leave no trace of your visit and take your litter home
- Keep dogs under effective control

**Enjoy** the outdoors

- Plan ahead and be prepared
- Follow advice and local signs

# MAPS & GRID REFERENCES

Ordnance Survey (OS) maps provide essential supporting detail, especially in locating parking at the start of walks. Relevant OS maps are:-

- Landranger No.166 Luton and Hertford, 1:50,000 scale
- Explorer No.182 St Albans and Hatfield, 1:25,000 scale
- More detailed maps, 1:10,000 scale, are available for inspection at public libraries

Of these, the Explorer range is preferred. These are subdivided into a "Grid" of 4cm squares, each representing one kilometre (km), and the squares can be subdivided into 10 smaller divisions for accuracy to within 100m. These identify the Grid References (GR) of all the features of an area and take the form of two letters and six digits.

The two letters represent a 100 km square area. For Explorer Map No.182 these letters are TL, which can therefore be disregarded, as all walks except No.24 are covered by this map. The six digits are quoted at the top of the walk instructions in this book. Walk No.24 also starts on OS Explorer Map No.182, but the southern section is covered by Map No.173 (and the 100 km square TQ).

Suppose you need to locate Toms Lane car park, Bedmond. The grid reference given is GR 095-035. Read the first two digits (09) along the top or bottom of the OS map to find the western edge of the one km square, followed by one more digit (5) to give the west-east position to within 100m. Then, read the next two digits (03) along one of the sides of the OS map to find the southern edge of the one km square, followed by 1 more digit (5) to give the south-north position to within 100m. The location of the car park is where the two lines cross.

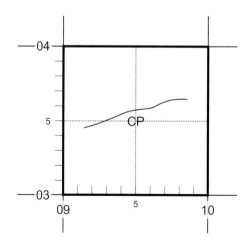

Note, not all "paths and tracks" shown on OS maps (or in this book) are public rights of way.

# LEGEND

| | |
|---|---|
| ———— | Motorway and Dual Carriageways |
| ═════ | Other Roads |
| = = = = = = | Track, Unmetalled Road, or Lane |
| - - - - - - - - | Path |
| --▶ --▶ --▶ | Route Arrows: Main - Black, Alternatives: A Red, B Blue |
| ———— | Railway |
| - - - o - - - o - - - | Overhead High Voltage Power Line (OHP) |
| † | Church |
| X | Signpost |
| ^ v < > | Waymark (only selected ones shown). Pointing in line of travel. Roundel colours are: footpath (yellow), bridleway (blue), byway (red) |
| G | Gate (of any kind, including "kissing", "motorcycle inhibitor") |
| FB | Footbridge |
| PH | Public House |
| L, R | The walker's left or right when walking the route |
| (N), (S), (E), (W) | Compass points (North, South, East, West) (may be combined; for example NE for North-East) |
| Km / m | Kilometres / metres |
| GR | Grid Reference (see section on map reading) |
| CP | Car Park |
| WC | Public Toilets (or 'free to the public') |
| Stile | Named as such on map |
| ☀ | View: symbol or named as such on map |

Leading the way in
sociable walking in and
around the St Albans
area since 1967

"Walking is Good For Your Health and Wellbeing"

# ST ALBANS & DISTRICT
# FOOTPATHS SOCIETY

offers :

- 2 to 3 weekly walks led by members
- Friendly companions   • Social events

### Find out more from :

www.stalbansfootpaths.org

stalbansfootpaths@gmail.com

**ST ALBANS & DISTRICT FOOTPATHS SOCIETY**

Reg. Charity No.1039715

7

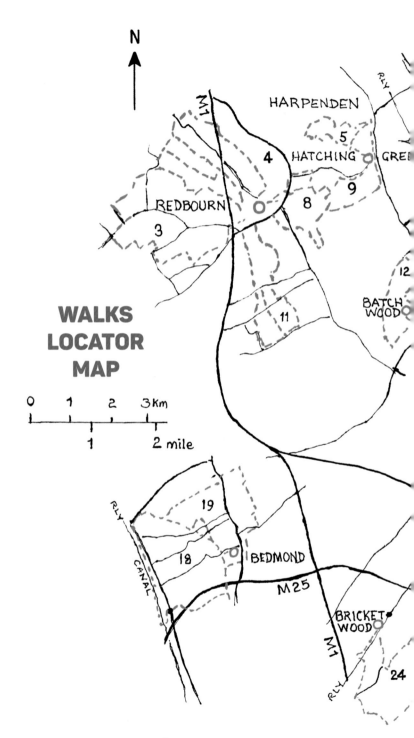

N

WALKS
LOCATOR
MAP

0    1    2    3 km

1         2 mile

HARPENDEN

5

4    HATCHING    GRE

8    9

REDBOURN

3

11

12

BATCH
WOOD

19

18    BEDMOND

M25

BRICKET
WOOD

24

M1

CANAL

RLY

RLY

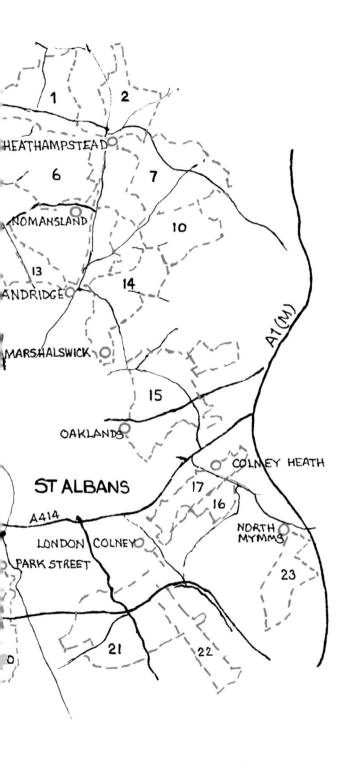

# CONTENTS

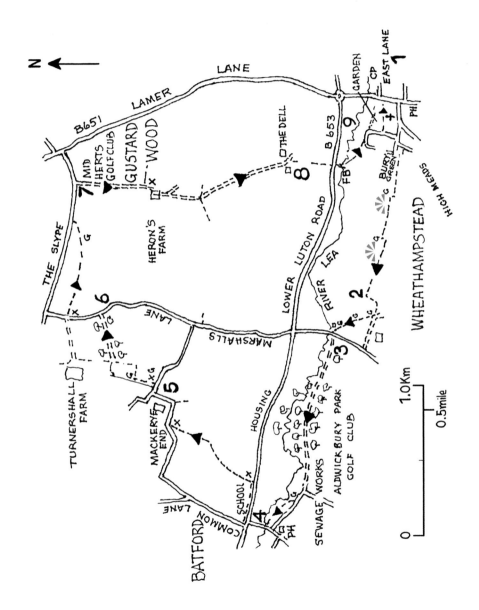

Total Distance 9.9km / 6.2 miles

# WHEATHAMPSTEAD, BATFORD, & GUSTARD WOOD

Park in public car park in East Lane, Wheathampstead *[POI 01]*, GR 178-141 *(beyond car park of The Bull [POI 14])*. *(Toilets at car park entrance)*

**1** From car park, turn R (W) to the High Street and cross road at the crossing. Turn L, then R at No.22 into alleyway. At footpath sign L, take path and cross churchyard *[POI 02]* to gate. Turn R into Bury Green, uphill past Ash Grove R, then L into High Meads. In a few metres take path R (W) at signpost and continue through two hedges and past seats *(here there are views across the valley)*.

**2** At cross-track, turn L then R to join a track. Go R (NW) through kissing gate and down path in field, with hedge L, to another kissing gate. Go through this *(note view of Leasey Bridge Farm and barn behind to R)* and cross field diagonally (NW) to gate by a bungalow. This leads to a lane *(Leasey Bridge Lane)* where turn R, then L onto bridleway *[POI 03]*.

**3** Continue (W) for 1.0km past golf course L to sewage works. Turn L down steps, then R under bridge into lane *(Marquis Lane)*. At first bend, turn R (NW) through kissing gate onto path across field to bridge *(note Marquis of Granby PH to L)*. Cross River Lea *[POI 04]*, turn R onto lane *(Crabtree Lane)* to B653 *(Lower Luton Road)*, *(note Batford [POI 05] is to L)*.

**4** Carefully cross road and turn R (E) onto pavement with school site *[POI 06]* on L. In 300m, at Wheathampstead sign, turn L (N) onto uphill path between hedges. This emerges onto lane where turn R, then L past Mackerye End *[POI 07]*.

**5** At T-junction, turn R and in 25m take footpath L (N). Follow path, then turn R around field with fence and hedge L, to cross-track between hedges. Turn R (E) along tree-lined track to lane *(Marshalls Heath Lane)*.

**6** Turn L (N) and opposite entrance to Turnershall Farm *[POI 08]*, turn R (E) at signpost along grassy track across a field. At field corner continue past allotments L onto track, to meet road *(The Slype)*. Turn R (E) to first crossroads *(Gustard Wood Common) [POI 09]*.

**7** At crossroads turn R (S) at sign *(Gustard Wood 23-1)* with cottages R *[POI 10]* and golf course L. Continue (S) on track leading to Heron's Farm *[POI 11]*. **EITHER** follow public right of way, turning R then L through farmyard and continue (S), **OR** use signed alternative onto track with barns R. Ignore bridleway R and track L, continuing (S) with power lines L. Ignore cross-path and continue under power lines to house *(The Dell)* in lane *(Rose Lane)*.

**8** Go through kissing gate R and take path (S) down field to B653 *(Lower Luton Road)*. Carefully cross road to asphalt path and go over the River Lea, bearing L (SE) to road *(Ash Grove)* and turn L past Bury Farm Cottages *[POI 12]*.

**9** Where this road turns R, go ahead (E) through gate onto bridleway *(with open space R)*. At far end, turn R (S) with the "Crinkle-Crankle" wall L *[POI 13]* *(with garden to L)*. At the end of this wall, turn L into churchyard and along path to High Street. Turn L, then use crossing back to East Lane and car park.

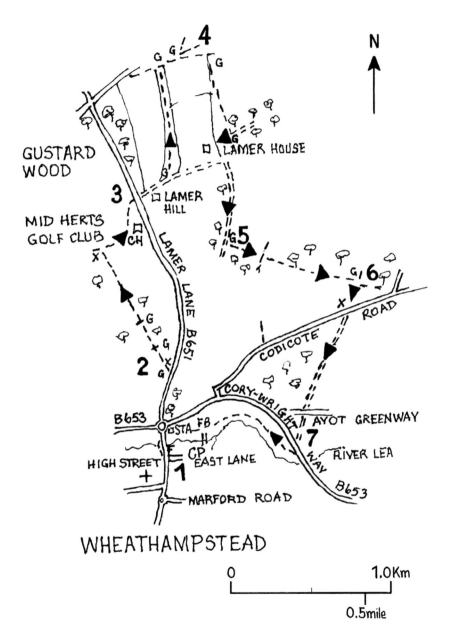

N

**4**

GUSTARD
WOOD

☐ LAMER HOUSE
G

**3** ☐ LAMER
HILL

MID HERTS
GOLF CLUB CH

LAMER LANE B651

**5**

**6**

ROAD

CODICOTE

**2**

CORY-WRIGHT

B653

STA FB
HIGH STREET CP
EAST LANE
+ **1**

AYOT GREENWAY

RIVER LEA

WAY

B653

MARFORD ROAD

**7**

WHEATHAMPSTEAD

0                    1.0Km

0.5mile

Total Distance 7.8km / 4.8 miles

# WHEATHAMPSTEAD, GUSTARD WOOD, & LAMER WOOD

Park in public car park in East Lane, Wheathampstead *[POI 01]*, GR 178-141 *(beyond car park of The Bull [POI 14])*. *(Toilets at car park entrance)*

**1** From car park turn R (W) to the High Street and cross road at the crossing. Turn R (N) and go along path *(Mill Walk)* between the River Lea mill stream L *[POI 04 & 14]* and small shops R. Continue to roundabout and cross road (N) to B651 *(Lamer Lane)*. In 200m, opposite wrought-iron gates, turn L at signpost through kissing gate.

**2** Take path (NW) to L of trees, then bear R to R of fence. Go through kissing gate and continue to another kissing gate L of telecoms mast. Enter golf course, keeping fence and hedge R to signposted cross-track. Turn R onto tarmac track, turning L (N) past club house R to T-junction and car park. Turn R on exit road, and at Guelders *(with its post box)*, cross Lamer Lane to signpost opposite.

**3** Continue past weather-boarded cottages onto asphalt road and turn R (NE). Pass Lamer Hill R and at far boundary of wooded garden R, turn L (N) through kissing gate onto path through Lamer Wood *(seasonal snowdrops and bluebells)*. Continue for 800m with fence R to boundary of woods. Go through kissing gate and turn R (E) with wood R, through another kissing gate (E) *(ignore gate L)*. Continue between wire fences through a further gate at corner of the wood R and to gate in fence *(do not go through gate)*.

**4** Turn R (S) with wire fence L to and through kissing gate in corner of field. *(Note fine avenue of trees on L)*. Turn R along track, through kissing gate onto asphalt road, and turn L (S). Where road bends R after Lamer House R, continue (S) on wide track for 550m, with high wire fence L, to kissing gate on L in woodland *(Lamer Park [POI 15])*.

**5** Turn L (E) through gate in high wire fence and along path on L edge of the wood with fence both sides past private cross-track. Bear L (NE then E) *(ignore track R)* through woodland, with avenue of trees R. At edge of the wood, continue (E) up a slope and through kissing gate in high wire fence.

**6** Turn R (S), keeping close to fence R to signpost at road *(Codicote Road)*. Cross road onto wide track (S) with wood R, then over the Ayot Greenway *[POI 16]* and under road bridge.

**7** Immediately after bridge, **EITHER** go up steps on R, then R onto fenced path, **OR** *(to avoid steps)* go 50m beyond bridge, turning sharp R (NW) at signpost and through gate onto the same fenced path. Continue (W) between fences with views of River Lea L, and through two gates. After a waymark just after a bench, take permissive path L beside river L. Cross footbridge over river onto asphalt path R and continue along lane *(Meads Lane)* to signposted path on R back to the car park.

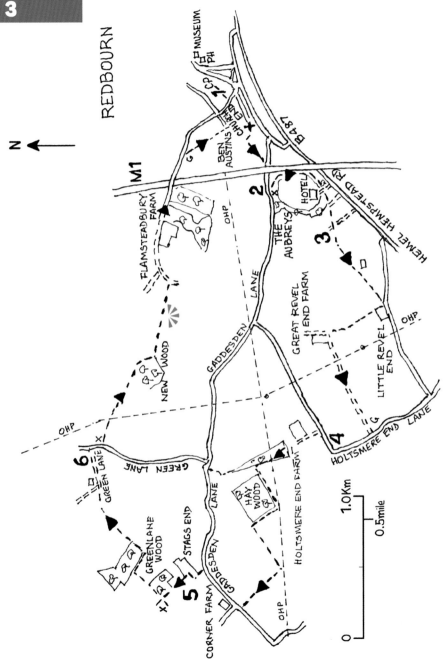

Total Distance 11.5km / 7.2 miles

# REDBOURN, THE AUBREYS, & GREENLANE WOOD

Park in car park on Redbourn Common by cricket pavilion *[POIs 17 & 18]*, GR 103-119

**1** Facing pavilion, turn L (SW) along asphalt path across the common. Cross road *(West Common)* into Church End *[POI 19]* and continue to gate at St Mary's Church *[POI 20]*. Take path with church R into churchyard. At first side path, turn R (NW) to kissing gate. Go through, turn L (SW) for 25m, then diagonally R across field to far corner and into road *(Gaddesden Lane)*. Cross road, turn R under M1 *[POI 21]* then onto path beside road, then L at signpost *(footpath 9)*.

**2** Follow this path *(S, then SW)* beside the M1, around The Aubreys R *[POI 22]*, through kissing gate and across hotel access road to path between hedges. Continue, bearing R (SW) along hedged path to meet cross-track. Turn R along track until next cross-track. Turn R then immediately L (SW) onto path between houses.

**3** Bear R (W) across field to some oak trees, where bear L (SW) with hedge R, then between fence L and hedge R. Pass farm L and house R to an open field, then cross to field corner, aiming for HV pylon on L. At field corner by Little Revel End *[POI 23]*, turn R (NW) with hedge and fence L, go through cross-hedge and up to L corner of hedge ahead. Turn L (SW) on farm track, continue under HV power lines to reach gate at lane *(Holtsmere End Lane)*. Turn R along lane and round bend to Holtsmere End.

**4** Turn L up lane *(a public right of way)*, past Holtsmere End Farm R and continue to gated path junction. Take footpath L (NW) *(footpath 46a, **NOT** bridleway 46)* through wood to wooden crossing barrier, go through, then turn L (SW) through hedge. Continue with Hay Wood R to another hedge gap, turn R (NW) onto bridleway with wood R. At end of wood, turn L (SW), follow path to cross-hedge, turn R (NW) and continue to lane *(Cupid Green Lane)*. Turn R (NE) along lane, then along Gaddesden Lane to Stags End Cottage Barn R, and cross road to signposted track.

**5** Take track L (NW) zig-zagging around house *(Stags End)* to paddock R, then through small copse to signposted cross-path. Turn R (NE) and continue with wood R, then downhill to Greenlane Wood. Turn R (SE) to corner of wood, then L (NE) uphill with wood L. Continue with hedge L to its end, then bear R across field to hedge gap. Turn R on track to meet lane *(Green Lane)*.

**6** Turn R, then in 50m at signpost *(footpath 40)*, turn L (SE) along path with hedge L. Go under HV power lines towards L corner of wood and continue with wood R. At far corner of wood, the track bears L between fields *(with a fine view towards St Albans)* to join cross-track. Turn L (NE) then R at next cross-track *(a bridleway)*. Turn R (E) past Flamsteadbury Farm, leading to lane *(Flamsteadbury Lane)*. Cross M1 then turn R (SE) at kissing gate onto signposted path *(footpath 21)*. At field corner turn L into road *(Ben Austins)*, then cross road *(West Common)* onto Redbourn Common and bear R back to cricket pavilion and car park.

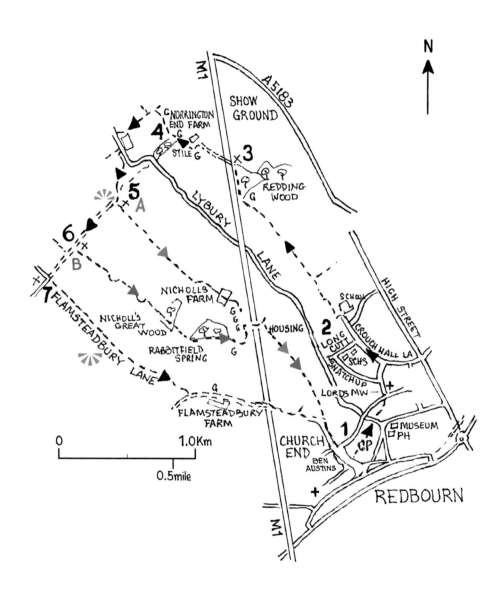

Total Distance 7.9km / 4.9 miles
Alternative A: 7.2km / 4.4 miles
Alternative B: 7.9km / 4.9 miles

# REDBOURN TOWARDS FLAMSTEAD

**Park in car park on Redbourn Common by cricket pavilion *[POIs 17 & 18]*, GR 103-119**

**1** Facing pavilion, turn R (NE) along asphalt path to Lybury Lane. Cross and bear L (N) on grassy path to road *(North Common)*. Cross road *(with bus stop to L)*, turn R then L (N) along Lords Meadow *(Methodist Church is to R)*. Turn L at Crouch Hall Lane, with school boundary on L and houses R. At Long Cutt, cross Crouch Hall Lane to asphalt path on R between houses R and trees L.

**2** At bend in road *(start of Black Horse Lane)*, cross and go into cul-de-sac opposite, with St Luke's School R. At end of cul-de-sac, continue on asphalt path between high hedges, turning L then R (NW). At signpost on L *(ignore asphalt path to L)* continue with school boundary R. Continue (NW) to and across fields, with M1 *[POI 21]* sign to L, and under HV power lines. At M1 boundary fence go through gate onto path between fence L and trees R to lane. Turn L (W) *(Herts Showground [POI 24] is to R)*.

**3** Go over M1 and after 150m at signpost *(just before house and Norrington End Farm)* turn L (SW) through gate on R of main gate. In 50m turn R (NW) through kissing gate and over stile in cross-fence. Continue downhill to corner of field.

**4** Go L through kissing gate, turn R downhill through gate. At the bottom, go through gates either side of fenced farm track, then turn L onto bridleway to lane. At the lane, turn L for 100m to signpost on R. Turn R, then L (S) up bridleway 54 to Redbourn *(ignore bridleway 27 to Trowley Bottom)*. Continue uphill to top and signpost for footpath 7 on L. **Alternative route A** starts here.

**5** Where track bears R (SW), note view R (N) towards Flamstead through wide field entrance. Continue between trees for 450m to signpost for footpath 38 on L. **Alternative route B** starts here.

**6** Continue on track (SW) for 400m to road corner with signpost for bridleway 39 on R.

**7** Turn L (SE) along bridleway for 1.8km, crossing open fields to Flamsteadbury Farm, around gate, then over M1. Continue along lane *(Flamsteadbury Lane)* until opposite Ben Austins R, then bear L over common, back to cricket pavilion and car park.

**A** **Alternative route A : *(total distance 7.2km / 4.4 miles)*.** At signpost for footpath 7 *(to Redbourn Common)*, turn L (SE) along track for 1.3km. This becomes an access road through Nicholls Farm. Cross over M1, go under HV power lines to signpost and waymark on R. Turn R along footpath with fence on L, then through gateway L. Follow path (SE) along boundary fence of housing to lane *(Flamsteadbury Lane)*. Bear L along lane until opposite Ben Austins R, then bear L over common, back to cricket pavilion and car park.

**B** **Alternative route B : *(total distance 7.9km / 4.9 miles)*.** At signpost for footpath 38 *(to Redbourn)*, turn L (SE) on path for 900m with hedge L. Where boundary of wood goes R, enter at waymark and follow clear, narrow path inside R edge of woods *(seasonal bluebells)*. After 600m emerge from woods on path with hedge L, through a hedge, then to far corner of field by power line. Go through gap in cross-hedge, then through kissing gate L. Cross field and through two more kissing gates, turning L (N) between fences then through kissing gate onto access road at signpost. Turn R, cross over M1, go under HV power lines to signpost and waymark R. Turn R along footpath with fence on L, then through gateway L. Follow path (SE) along boundary fence of housing to lane *(Flamsteadbury Lane)*. Bear L along lane until opposite Ben Austins R, then bear L over common, back to cricket pavilion and car park.

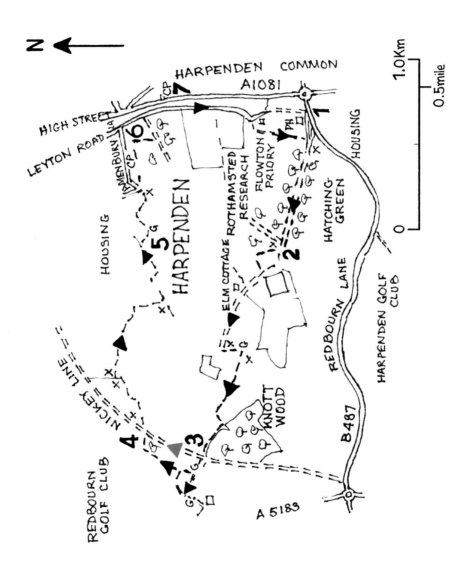

Total Distance 7.8km / 4.8 miles
Alternative: 0.8km / 0.5 mile shorter

# HATCHING GREEN, ROTHAMSTED, & HARPENDEN

**Park at Hatching Green off B487, GR 134-130**

**1** Go (W) 600m along road into Rothamsted to junction with tree-lined avenue R.

**2** A few metres after junction, bear R through wooden fence at bridleway signpost, then with wire fence R. At end of fence, turn L with hedge R to signpost by Elm Cottage. Cross road and bear L (NW) to join farm road with Elm Cottage R *(Rothamsted Manor [POI 28] is to L)*. Follow road until it turns R, where turn L along signposted bridleway, then R at next signpost. Continue along track, across cross-track towards wood *(Knott Wood, seasonal bluebells)*. The track bears R at wood and continues (NW) with wood on L to the Nickey Line *[POI 29]*.

**3** An Alternative route starts here *(shortens walk by 0.8km / 0.5 mile)*. Turn R along Nickey Line to signposted cross-path, then turn R.

**OTHERWISE**, cross the Nickey Line and follow path (NW) between fences. Where path meets track bear L, then where track turns L, turn R through kissing gate R. Follow path over pasture and through another kissing gate. Continue with fence L, then between hedges to edge of wood and kissing gate L. Keep on path through wood, with golf course L. Near end of wood, turn R to emerge onto golf course, and bear R (E) to path between hedges through a barrier. Continue along field edge to cross Nickey Line again.

**4** Continue (E) along well-marked path with hedge R. Where path meets farm road, turn L. In 20m *(at signpost)* turn R (E) into field with hedge R *(ignore paths to R of hedge and diagonally across field)*. At the end of field turn R with hedge R and housing L. Emerge into field, turn L and follow round to park entrance and notice board *(footpath 13 entrance)*. Keep hedge L, go past cricket pavilion on L.

**5** Continue with hedge L until a second pavilion R. Keeping just to L of pavilion, go through gap in hedge on L onto gravel track. Follow track past tennis courts L and sports field R to Amenbury Lane car park with swimming pool R.

**6** Turn R past swimming pool to tree-lined avenue, then L (NE) to park exit and road *(Leyton Road)*. Turn R (S) along road past the Old House L *(former Bull Inn [POI 47])* then Silver Cup PH.

**7** After Sir Joseph's Walk note the Rothamsted Memorial outside Rothamsted Research *[POI 27]*. Continue along West Common road. After Pimlico Place *[POI 30]*, take signposted path *(footpath 8)* on R (S) past Flowton Priory L *[POI 31]* back to Hatching Green. *(The White Horse PH is in Redbourn Lane to the L).*

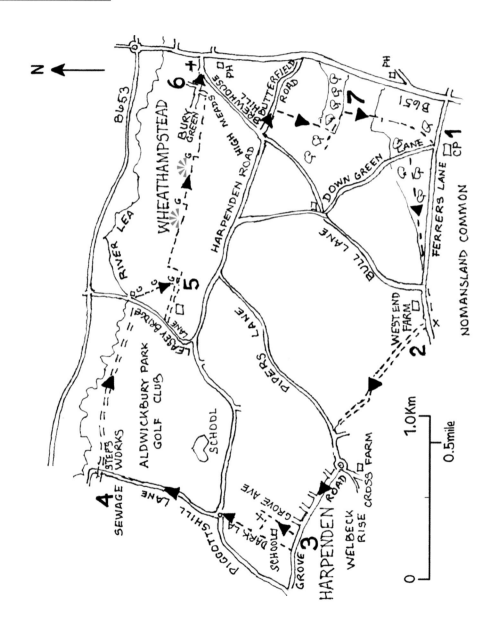

Total Distance 9.5km / 5.9 miles

# NOMANSLAND, HARPENDEN, & WHEATHAMPSTEAD

Park in car park on Nomansland Common *[POI 32]*, Ferrers Lane, opposite junction with Down Green Lane, GR 171-124

**1** Cross Ferrers Lane, go (N) along Down Green Lane for 200m to cross-track *(bridleway)*. Turn L (W) between two oak posts into woodland. Avoiding forks, follow path for 800m to Ferrers Lane. Go past junction with lane *(Bull Lane)*, cross Ferrers Lane, go past gate and turn R onto path leading to boardwalk. Follow this back to Ferrers Lane.

**2** At signpost, cross Ferrers Lane and take wide track opposite (NW). Continue with hedge L then R to road junction with Pipers Lane. Cross road and go (W) on pavement R, passing Welbeck Rise L *(Cross Farm is to L [POI 33])*, then bear R along Grove Road past several roads to footpath on R after Grove Avenue.

**3** Turn R (N) along path, passing school L, uphill to signposted path L *(footpath 28)*. Turn L along path through trees between school L and allotments R. Before junction with road, turn R onto path through trees and emerge onto lane *(Piggottshill Lane)*, where turn R (N) to small roundabout. Cross onto L pavement and continue past Aldwickbury Park Golf Club R, where lane narrows and goes downhill.

**4** After the sewage works, and before the old railway bridge *[POI 03]*, go up steps R onto track and turn R (E). Continue for 1.0km to Leasey Bridge Lane *(view of the River Lea to L [POI 04])*, then turn R up lane for 20m. Turn L up 'Little Croft' bungalow drive, through kissing gate and bear L (S) up field *(note view of Leasey Bridge Farm and barn to R)*. Go through second kissing gate, then with hedge R, through third kissing gate onto track.

**5** Turn L (E) along track with fence on each side, turning L round a field, then turn R (E) at waymark with hedge L. Continue on track then path past seats and through two hedges *(gap in first, gate in second)* to edge of housing. The path becomes an alley to meet road *(High Meads)*. Turn L then R onto road *(Bury Green)* and go downhill into Church Street.

**6** Turn R (SW) and go up Brewhouse Hill *[POI 34]*, to near top of the hill, turning L (E) into Butterfield Road. In 130m, at signpost R *(to Nomansland)* turn R (S) on path between houses. Continue for 400m through woodland, then turn L (E) at waymark along inside edge of wood *(do not exit wood at this point)*. Continue to power line pole.

**7** At this pole turn R (S) along R edge of field following the power line. The path enters woodland past a notice stating "Nomansland". Continue (S, W, and S) following directions on waymarks through woods to Lanman Cottage. Ignore track R, continue straight ahead (SW) through woods back to Ferrers Lane and car park.

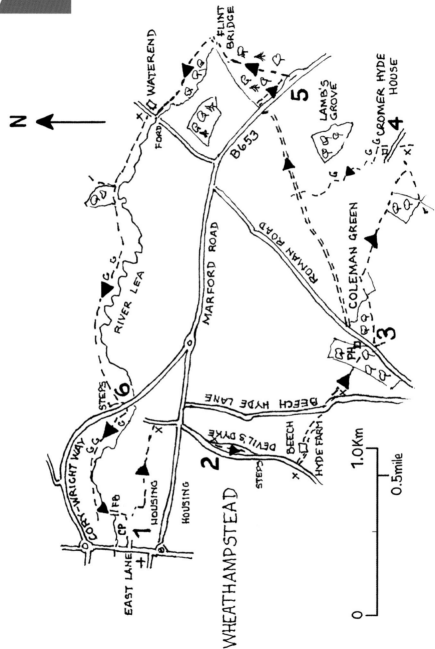

Total Distance 10.1km / 6.3 miles

# WHEATHAMPSTEAD, COLEMAN GREEN, & WATEREND

Park in public car park in East Lane, Wheathampstead, *[POI 01]* GR 178-141 *(beyond car park of The Bull [POI 14]). (Toilets at car park entrance)*

**1** From car park, turn L (E). Just past Mead Hall L, bear R and continue up East Lane then L onto path into recreation ground L. Follow tarmac path, turn R past football pitch L. Turn L, with tennis courts R and along path with hedge R. Continue between fence L and hedge R to road, then turn R uphill to Marford Road. Carefully cross and continue up Dyke Lane to entrance to Devil's Dyke L *[POI 35]*.

**2** Enter and keep to bottom of the dyke. Towards end, turn R up steps at Herts Way signpost. The path curves R at top, back into Dyke Lane. Turn L along lane to signposted path to Beech Hyde Farm. Turn L into farm on poplar-lined track *(keeping to L track)* between farm buildings, then L and R to gate and road junction. Turn R and in a few metres L at Herts Way signpost. Continue uphill across field to a wood. Go through wood and exit by cottage L onto the green at signpost *(with John Bunyan PH to L [POI 36])*. Turn R (SW) for 100m to waymark, then L to cross lane.

**3** Turn L along lane for 10m then take L of two paths into woods. Keep inside R edge of woods to and through gap, with woods now on R. Bear R at end of wood, then uphill, bearing L to second group of holly bushes. Bear R keeping hedge L, over cross-path, continue with wood R to a gap. Go through gap with hedge L to waymarked cross-path. Turn L through hedge and across field to Cromer Hyde House.

**4** Cross lane, bear R (N) on waymarked path with hedge L to and through kissing gate L. Go across field with hedge L and through kissing gate to R of stables. Continue beside raised bank and wire fence, through kissing gate, then downhill with hedge L onto sunken track. Turn R down track. At the end, turn L up to road *(B653, Marford Road)*. Carefully cross, turn L to pass end of barrier on far side of road, then turn sharply R onto path to lay-by in 300m.

**5** At centre of lay-by the path starts through gap in fence into woods. Go (N) downhill across Flint Bridge *[POI 37]* over River Lea *[POI 04]*, then turn L (NW) along path with fence L. This follows river L and emerges onto lane at Waterend with ford L. Turn R, then L (W) opposite large house *(Waterend House [POI 38])*. The gravel bridleway follows river with hedge L. In 500m at a bend, continue ahead (W) on path for 700m with wood R, then with hedge L to and through kissing gate. Continue with fence L through another kissing gate, then bear L into water meadows. Continue to signposted gate by road.

**6** Turn R along fenced path, then turn L down steps and L under bridge. Immediately after bridge, **EITHER** go up steps on R, then R on to fenced path, **OR** *(to avoid steps)* go 50m beyond bridge, turning sharp R (NW) at signpost and through gate onto the same fenced path. Continue (W) between fences *(views of River Lea L)* through two gates. Just after a bench, at waymark take permissive path L beside river L. Cross footbridge over river onto asphalt path R and continue along lane *(Meads Lane)* to signposted path on R back to the car park.

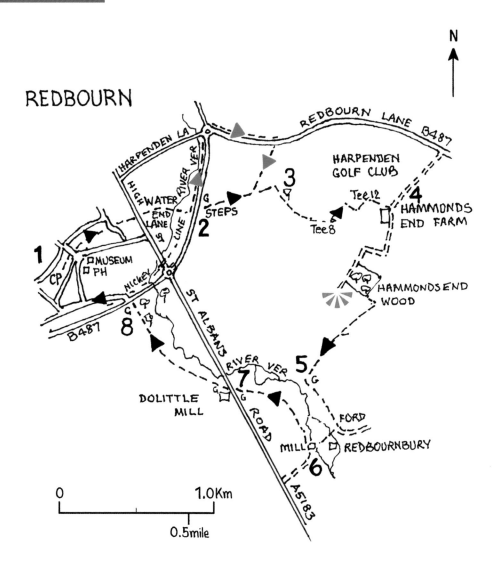

REDBOURN

N

Total Distance 7.0km / 4.4 miles
Alternative: 1.4km / 0.9 mile longer

# REDBOURN, & REDBOURNBURY

Park in car park on **Redbourn Common** by cricket pavilion *[POIs 17 & 18]*, GR 103-119

**1** Facing pavilion, turn R (NE) along asphalt path to Lybury Lane. Cross road, keep straight ahead to road *(The Common)*. Cross and continue (E) along path between brick walls *(The Ruins)* and past Cumberland House L *[POI 39]* to High Street. Cross to Waterend Lane opposite. Go down this lane, bearing R towards and over ford *(use footbridge if flooded)* of the River Ver *[POI 40]*. In 70m path turns L then R. Pass path L continuing with green metal fence L to steps down to the Nickey Line *[POI 29]*.

**2** An Alternative route starts here *(in muddy conditions; extends route by 1.4km / 0.9 mile)*. Turn L on Nickey Line to roundabout. Follow signs across two roads, using islands, then turn R along pavement. Go L up slope then turn R up bank *(a right of way)* to go beside and above Redbourn Lane towards Harpenden. Continue for 400m to waymark then turn R down to road and carefully cross road to footpath, zig-zagging up to barrier. The right of way path continues across the field, **OR** *(if this is unusable)*, turn L (E) and follow field edge around three sides to power line pole, then continue as above.

**OTHERWISE**, turn L then R through kissing gate to A5183 by-pass. Carefully cross road and go up steps opposite, through kissing gate to field path. Continue (E) uphill along path parallel with power line through hedge gap by power pole. Continue ahead with hedge R to waymark at woods, then turn R 20m to power line pole.

**3** Turn L by waymark then R (SE) through hedge. Continue through trees bordering Harpenden Golf Club *[POI 41]* to emerge onto edge of course. Turn R then L (E) around tee-8 *(Ramblers Risk)*, and continue close to hedge R past green 8. 25m past tee-9, turn R at waymark into trees, follow path to emerge at tee-12. Follow along gravel track for 20m, then turn R with fence R to concealed kissing gate. Cross small field, keeping fence R to second kissing gate into lane.

**4** Turn R (S) past Hammonds End House *[POI 42]* and farm R with pond and barns L. Continue on track which soon turns R and then L (SW) with hedge and wood L. At next corner of wood is a seat *(view to Redbournbury)*. Turn L (SE) along wood boundary to bottom of field, then turn R (SW) with hedge L, then R, to gate and farm access track.

**5** Turn L (SE) along this track with trees R to ford. Turn R, cross footbridge next to ford, and continue with Redbournbury *[POI 43]* on L. Cross second footbridge, then road bridge over river to Redbournbury Mill R *[POI 44]*.

**6** Turn R (N) at signpost and go through mill forecourt, keeping to L of mill building *(not through overflow car park to L)*. Continue along hedged track through two kissing gates. Path continues (N, then NW) with views of river, to A5183 at gate.

**7** Carefully cross road to Dolittle Mill *[POI 45]*, go through small gate and cross forecourt through kissing gate R, continue (NW) with fence R and hedge L. At end of hedge and fence bear R (N) along clear path with hedge R past gate. Cross bridge *(over River Red [POI 46])* to Redbourn by-pass *(B487)*.

**8** Carefully cross by-pass, turn L (W) along Chequer Lane passing the Nickey Line. Cross East Common road, then bear R onto path past two sides of children's play area to gravel path, road and back to car park.

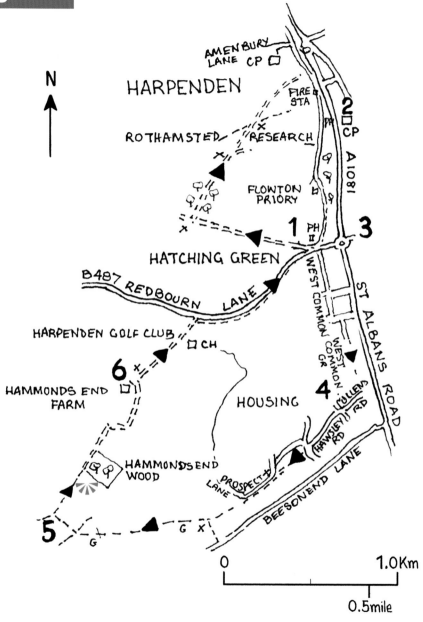

N

HARPENDEN

Total Distance 8.2km / 5.1 miles

# HATCHING GREEN, HARPENDEN, & HAMMONDS END

### Park at Hatching Green off B487, GR 134-130

**1** Go (W) 600m along road into Rothamsted to junction with tree-lined avenue R. Turn R along avenue, then track, to cross-track and gate. Continue along avenue into Rothamsted Park *[POI 27]*, then to main entrance at road *(Leyton Road)*. Turn R (S) to pass Old House L *(former Bull Inn [POI 47])* then Silver Cup PH L.

**2** Continue (S) along road that becomes West Common *(note Rothamsted Memorial outside Rothamsted Research [POI 27])*. Go past attractive group of cottages R *(Pimlico Place [POI 30])* *(ignoring signposted footpath 8 R)*, with Flowton Priory R *[POI 31]* to cross Redbourn Lane at the crossing.

**3** Continue (S) along West Common *(a mix of roads and paths)*. At West Common Way, turn L and R to West Common Grove. Just before the end take a clear, but unsigned path L (SE) at the turning area. At junction with an access road leading to Maple Cottages, turn R (SW).

**4** Pass end of the cottages L. Where path turns L, go through gate ahead into Collens Road. Continue into and along Hawsley Road *(ignore side roads)*. At The Deerings continue on grassy path *(signposted footpath 5)* along rear of housing, then with road to R. Continue across a field to a signpost with path L from lane *(Beesonend Lane)*. Bear R (W) along clear track across field. Go through kissing gate in fence, downhill through kissing gate in hedge then to cross-track at gap in cross-hedge.

**5** Cross track onto path for 160m with hedge R to small clump of trees. Turn R (NE) uphill with hedge R to corner of wood *(Hammondsend Wood)* and seat with views to Redbournbury. Continue uphill with wood R. At cross-track, turn R then L passing large barn R. Continue (NE, then N) past Hammonds End Farm and Hammonds End House L *[POI 42]*.

**6** Bear R (NE) along access road with Harpenden Golf Club *[POI 41]* either side, then past the clubhouse R to road *(B487 Redbourn Lane)*. Bear R (E) on pavement to Hatching Green and back to start. *(The White Horse PH is ahead in Redbourn Lane)*.

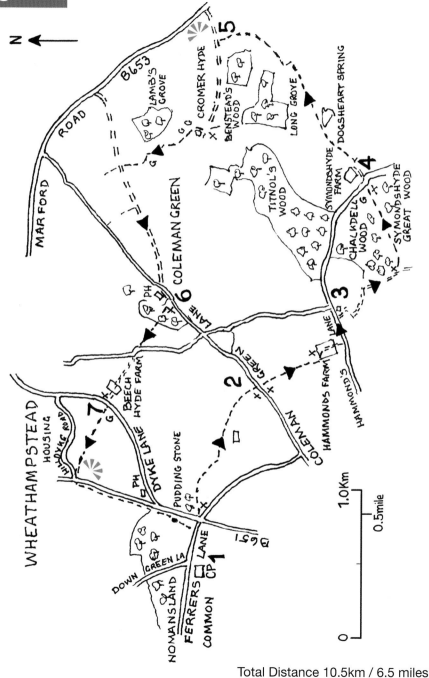

Total Distance 10.5km / 6.5 miles

# NOMANSLAND, SYMONDSHYDE, & COLEMAN GREEN

**Park in car park on Nomansland Common, *[POI 32]*, Ferrers Lane, opposite Down Green Lane, GR 171-124**

**1** Go R (E) along common beside Ferrers Lane towards crossroads with B651. Cross Ferrers Lane, then B651 and follow waymarked path through trees. This soon becomes a clear bridleway leading to lane *(Coleman Green Lane, a Roman road)*.

**2** Cross lane and continue (SE) along bridleway into farm track leading to Hammonds Farm. Follow track through two hedges, then bear L towards farm buildings and follow signs between farm buildings to access road then lane *(Hammonds Lane)*. Turn L (NE) up lane.

**3** At Meadow Lodge turn R (SE) onto gravel access track *(signposted byway to Fairfolds Lane)*. The track turns R then L to Symondshyde Great Wood. Turn R (S) on track for 250m along boundary fence with wood L to junction with waymarked track L. Turn sharp L (E then NE) along track to lane at gate.

**4** Turn R (SE) along this lane for 25m *(ignore first path on L)* then turn L (NE) along access road to Symondshyde Farm. Continue (NE) around gate, following track, passing farm and house on L into field with small pond R. Continue (NE) along field margin with bushes on R to small wood on R *(Dogsheart Spring)*, then with hedge on R, head for lone tree and waymarked hedge corner. Continue (NE) with hedge L to waymark at hedge from R, then cross a field towards L end of a line of trees. At cross-track *(R to Cromerhyde Farm)*, go forward (N) along track to lane *(Cromer Hyde Lane)*, *(look R for view of Brocket Hall [POI 48])*.

**5** Turn L (W) on lane to signpost opposite Cromer Hyde House. Bear R (N) beside hedge, past house L through kissing gate L. Go across field with hedge L through second kissing gate to R of stables. Continue (NW) beside raised bank and wire fence past oak trees L, through kissing gate then downhill with hedge L to sunken track. Turn L (W) up this track, crossing another track and passing the so-called John Bunyan Chimney R *[POI 36]*. At junction with lane *(Coleman Green Lane)*, cross road onto track, turn L (SW) and pass John Bunyan PH *(and Coleman Green Cottages)* on R.

**6** At signpost turn R (NW) with cottages R into and through woods. Continue across field on path onto lane at bend, then R along lane past cottage on L. After 40m, at sharp R bend, go onto track (NW) to Beech Hyde Farm and along its poplar-lined access road to junction with lane, then onto field path opposite and through gate.

**7** The path continues (NW) to housing with boundary fence R *(look back for views S and E)*, then into Hilldyke Road at junction with the B651. Cross and take path L (S) downhill beside road onto Nomansland Common. Continue beside road past cricket field and boundary pudding stone *[POI 49]* and cross Ferrers Lane, then turn R back to car park.

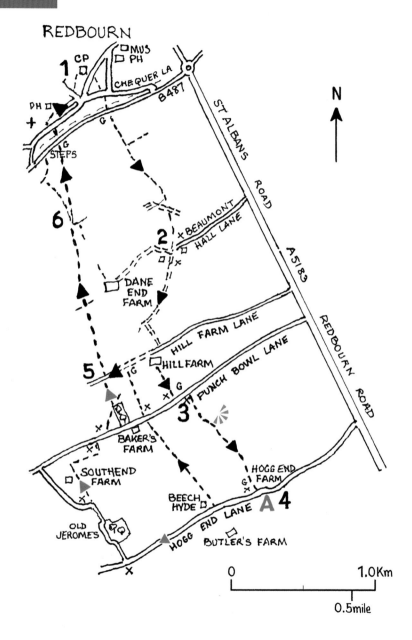

Total Distance 8.1km / 5.0 miles
Alternative: 2.4km / 1.5 miles longer

# REDBOURN, & HOGG END LANE

Park in car park on Redbourn Common by cricket pavilion *[POIs 17 & 18]*, GR 103-119

**1** Cross the road, turn R past building, then L (S) on path with children's play area L. Cross road *(Chequer Lane)* and continue between housing *(signposted to Nickey Line)*. Use steps to cross gravel track *(the Nickey Line [POI 29])*. Carefully cross by-pass *(B487)* and go up steps to kissing gate. Continue (S) to field corner and waymark, then through gap in hedge, with hedge L to corner of next field at foot of slope, go through gap in hedge. Bear slightly R up slope, heading for tall trees at top R, to field corner and lane *(Beaumont Hall Lane)*.

**2** Turn R along lane past White Cottage L. After 70m, bear L down a waymarked green lane passing New Cottage R. Stay on winding lane *(ignoring side paths R)*, to lane *(Hill Farm Lane)*, then turn R to Hill Farm. Turn L (S) onto farm access road, then after 10m turn R with farm buildings L and hay barn R to stile in fence L. Cross stile and turn L, passing farmhouse L, cross another stile to join grassy track with hedge R. Continue (S) to gate onto lane *(Punch Bowl Lane), (to R is M1 [POI 21] and Buncefield Oil Storage Depot [POI 50])*.

**3** Turn L along lane for 90m, then at signpost turn R onto path. Follow hedge R (S) to its end, then bear L (SE). Cross open field, heading for a group of trees to R of St Albans Abbey in the distance *(view to S across St Albans City)*, until waymark is seen at L end of hedge. Continue (S) along field track with hedge L to lane *(Hogg End Lane; note Hogg End Farm L)*.

**4** An Alternative route starts here *(extends route by 2.4km / 1.5 miles)*. At Hogg End Lane, turn R (SW) along this lane for 1.2km, then at cottages turn R along lane *(signposted Old Jeromes)*, passing Old Jeromes to R. The lane turns R, then L. Where lane next turns L, go through signposted gap in hedge and continue along path to farm track, passing Southend Farm L. At farm boundary, turn R (NE) across field parallel to power line L heading to white topped waymark on L of hedge. At hedge turn L (NW) to lane *(Punch Bowl Lane)*. Turn R along lane for 50m to signpost L just before house. Enter field and cross diagonally (NE) to corner of a small wood. Bear L (N) downhill to waymark post in hedge gap and cross sunken track to continue.

**OTHERWISE**, turn R (SW) along lane for 400m, then turn R (N) opposite Butler's Farm *(noting Beech Hyde to L)*. This track goes (N) for 600m with hedge L past several waymarks to old chalk pit on L, *(ahead to L is a whitewashed house called Baker's Farm)*. The path continues (N) across open field to gap and signpost in lane *(Punch Bowl Lane)*. Cross to signpost opposite, continue towards power poles and waymark near corner of fenced paddock R. Bear R through kissing gate across paddock, then over stile onto sunken track. Turn L (W) for 200m to waymark, then turn R (N).

**5** Cross field past two trees ahead to waymark at hedge. The path goes (N) with hedge R. At four-way path junction, with Dane End Farm NE, the path continues with hedge R. After 150m go through cross-hedge and continue with hedge R.

**6** After 450m, when a track comes in from R, go through gap in hedge and bear slightly R (N) diagonally across field heading to R of large tree. Go through another gap in hedge, continuing to field corner. Follow fence to kissing gate, then down steps and carefully cross by-pass *(B487)*.

**7** Go up steps, cross Nickey Line, then go (N) along short path between fences to road *(Hemel Hempstead Road)*. Cross and turn R to St Mary's Church *[POI 20]*. Enter churchyard, bearing R (NE) to gateway into Church End *(note old cottages and Hollybush PH [POI 19])*. Continue on asphalt path, cross road *(West Common)* back to cricket pavilion and car park.

CHILDWICK GREEN

LODGE

**5**

GREEN WOOD

**6**

CHILDWICK BURY HOUSE

HARPENDEN ROAD A1081

SCHOOL

SPORTS FIELD **1**

CP

HIGH OAKS

TOULMIN DRIVE

BATCH WOOD

GREEN LANE

LADIES GROVE WOOD

CH

**4**

BATCHWOOD HALL

FRANCIS AVE

GOLF COURSE

**2**

BATCHWOOD DRIVE

ST ALBANS

**3**

A5183

N

0       1.0Km

0.5mile

Total Distance 6.3km / 3.9 miles

# BATCH WOOD, & CHILDWICK GREEN

**Park in sports ground car park in Toulmin Drive, St Albans**
**GR 143-095**

**1** From car park, cross road to pavement, turn R (S) along Toulmin Drive with wood *(Batch Wood)* on R. Where the road turns sharp L at No.18, cross to bridleway signpost opposite. Continue then turn L for 250m around open space to signposted gap in hedge *(bridleway 1 to Batchwood Drive).*

**2** Turn R (SW) through gap and continue across golf course. Cross access road *(to Batchwood Hall [POI 51])* and follow waymarks across golf course onto exit road by signpost *(bridleway 88).*

**3** Turn R along this road, go round a R bend and in 70m turn L at signpost *(bridleway 2).* This soon turns R (N) with hedge R along boundary of the golf course. Continue along this path across field to L corner of wood *(Ladies Grove Wood).*

**4** Continue (N) along fenced path beside edge of wood, onto access road, which then passes Childwick Bury House R *[POI 52]* and leads to Childwick Green *[POI 53].*

**5** Near the pump in front of St Mary's Church L, turn R (SE) along road lined with rhododendron bushes. This bends L, then meets the road *(A1081 Harpenden Road)* by Childwick Lodge. Turn R (SE) onto pavement and continue for 300m to Hawkswick Lodge Farm *(signposted bridleway 1).*

**6** Turn R (SW) at farm entrance and along gravel track with fruit bushes R to signpost. Bear R to wooden gate in R corner of field. Go through gate and along a fenced track between hedges to emerge at sports field. Turn L (SE) on bridleway with hedge L through hedge R, then with school L and sports field R back to car park.

**NOTE:** There are many entrances, internal paths with various waymarks, and large oaks in Batch Wood. Other routes can be found to vary the walk.

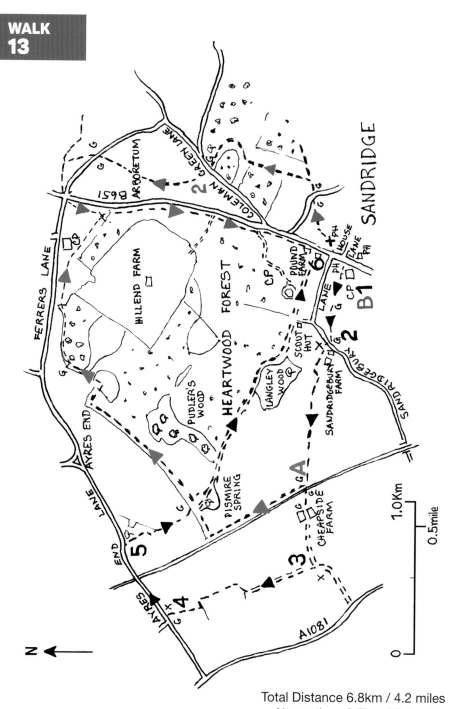

Total Distance 6.8km / 4.2 miles
Alternative: 3.7km / 2.3 miles

# SANDRIDGE, &
# HEARTWOOD FOREST

Park **(a)** in Spencer Meadows car park in Sandridge *[POI 54]* by village hall,
GR 169-104, *(where there are toilets)*
OR    **(b)** in Heartwood Forest car park, GR 168-108. To L of car park, go
through gate in hedge onto track. Turn L, through Pound Farm
to road. Turn R to Item 1

**NOTE:**  Many gates on either side of the route provide access to Heartwood Forest *[POI 55]*. There are numerous walks in Heartwood Forest; Alternative route A is given below. Another alternative, route B, is shown on the map, but not described here *(this goes through the recently planted arboretum and community orchard)*. Not all paths are rights of way.

**1** From rear of car park go past children's play area (W) along fence R of football pitch through kissing gate.  Follow right hand power line through second kissing gate and continue following power line through third signposted kissing gate and across lane *(Sandridgebury Lane)*.  Opposite, a bridleway *(signposted Childwick Green)* continues (W) between fences then hedges for 1.0km to bridge over railway *[POI 56]*. Alternative route A starts here.

**2** Alternative route A: *(total distance 3.7km / 2.3 miles)*.  Before bridge over railway, turn R (NW) up through gate.  Enter Heartwood Forest, with railway track L for 850m to gate, then turn R (E) with hedge L.  Go through two gates, crossing a bridleway.  Bear L (NE) for 1.0km to hedge, then turn R uphill to LH corner of wood *(Round Wood)*.  Turn L and continue with hedge L to kissing gate to enter Nomansland Common *[POI 32]*.  Turn R (E) over the common to the B651.  Turn R (S) with main road on L up to edge of common, and signpost at track *(bridleway 32)*.  Continue on track to Sandridge, then along pavement back to **starts (a)** and **(b)**.

**OTHERWISE,** cross bridge and go through farm gate.  Bear R (NW) through farm gate ahead and between farm buildings onto access road of Cheapside Farm. Turn R (W) and in 400m where road bears L, turn R (N) at signpost onto track.

**3** Go downhill with hedge L past plantation L with hedge R to the bottom. Where track turns L, bear R for a few metres with hedge L, then turn L through gap in hedge. Continue (N) uphill with hedge L, into lane *(Ayres End Lane)* by gate.

**4** Turn R along lane, passing houses L and over railway bridge.  Where road bears R, take bridleway R (S) at signpost.

**5** This bridleway continues for 2.6km, first parallel to the railway R (S), then (SE) past Langley Wood and Scout Hut R.  The bridleway also passes Heartwood Forest car park on L, **start (b)**, then goes through Pound Farm *[POI 57]* to road *(B651 Sandridge High Street)*.

**6** Turn R (SW), noting St. Leonard's Church on L *[POI 58]*, back to car park, **start (a)**.

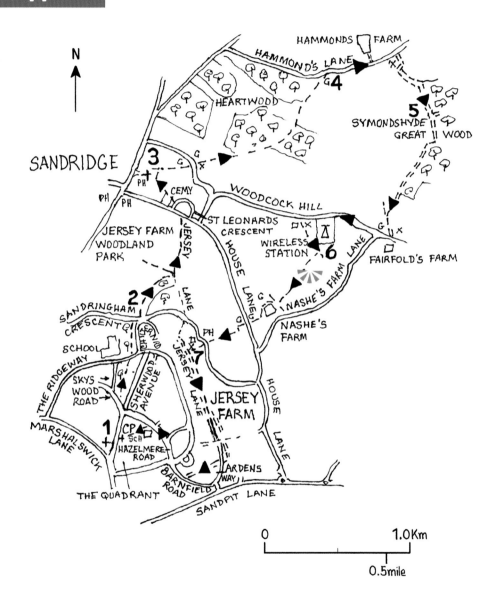

N

SANDRIDGE

HAMMONDS FARM

HAMMOND'S LANE

**4**

HEARTWOOD

**5**

SYMONDSHYDE
GREAT WOOD

**3**

PH

CEMY

PH

PH

WOODCOCK HILL

ST LEONARDS
CRESCENT

JERSEY FARM
WOODLAND
PARK

JERSEY

HOUSE LANE

WIRELESS
STATION

**6**

FAIRFOLD'S FARM

NASHE'S FARM LANE

SANDRINGHAM
CRESCENT

**2**

LANE

PH

NASHE'S FARM LANE

NASHE'S
FARM

SCHOOL

THE RIDGEWAY

SKYS
WOOD
ROAD

SHERWOOD AVENUE

JERSEY LANE

**7**

JERSEY
FARM

HOUSE LANE

MARSHALSWICK
LANE

**1**

CP
SCH

HAZELMERE
ROAD

BARNFIELD ROAD

ARDENS
WAY

THE QUADRANT

SANDPIT LANE

0                                   1.0Km

0.5mile

Total Distance 9.7km / 6.0 miles

# MARSHALSWICK, SANDRIDGE, & SYMONDSHYDE

**Park in Sherwood Avenue Recreation Ground car park *[POI 59]***
**GR 169-088**

**1** From car park entrance, cross road and turn R along Sherwood Avenue. Bear L into Skys Wood Road and cross. In 50m, at signpost by No.41, turn R (N) along path and enter wood *(Bentsley Spinney)*. Keep fence L and exit wood at alley and cross road *(The Ridgeway)*. Continue (N) on tree-lined track *(with boundary fence of school L)* to road junction *(Chiltern Road to R and Sandringham Crescent L)*.

**2** Cross Chiltern Road and continue (E) for 50m, then cross Sandringham Crescent at island. Ignore track R and enter Jersey Farm Woodland Park *[POI 60]* past memorial. Bear R (NE) on path with trees R to meet track *(Jersey Lane)*, then turn L (N) down to road *(House Lane)*. Carefully cross road, turn L (NW), then R (NE) at St Leonard's Crescent. In 50m, to R of No.3, turn L onto asphalt path with boundary fence on L. Go past small play area R then cemetery L and through barrier to St Leonard's Church *[POI 58]*. Bear R (N) past church to NE corner of churchyard.

**3** Cross lane at barrier, and turn R (E) along path with housing L and hedge R. Cross road through gates onto wide grassy track opposite *(note Heartwood Forest L [POI 55])*. Continue across open fields to and through wood. Continue (E then NE) into field with ditch and hedge L to lane *(Hammonds Lane)*.

**4** Turn R up lane for 600m past Hammonds Farm L. At Meadow Lodge turn R (SE) onto gravel access track *(signposted byway to Fairfolds Lane)*. The track turns R, then L to Symondshyde Great Wood. Turn R (S) on track for 250m along boundary fence with wood L to junction with waymarked track L.

**5** Ignore track L, continuing along track through woods. In 200m turn R at waymark, then after 50m turn L (SW). Keep inside R edge of wood until exiting with field R, then with hedge L. This leads to kissing gate and road *(Woodcock Hill)* by Fairfold's Farm. Turn R (W) along road to fork in road. Turn R (NW) for 600m up Woodcock Hill passing DSTL Wireless Station L *[POI 61]*. Just before cottages, turn L (S) at signpost onto path to open field. Turn L (E) with fence L to waymark at field boundary, then turn R (SW) *(view (S) to Shenley water tower [POI 62])*.

**6** Continue downhill (SW) with fence L to cross-track and through kissing gate opposite. Bear R downhill past Nashe's Farm, then bear L down through kissing gate onto road *(House Lane)*. Carefully cross and go through kissing gate onto track. Turn L, then R (SW) *(with adventure playground R)* onto asphalt path uphill between housing *(ignore paths to L)*. Cross road *(Sandringham Crescent)*, then in 150m meet a tree-lined cross-track *(Jersey Lane)*.

**7** Turn L (S) on track between housing across signposted bridleway. Follow track, turn R (W) across road *(Ardens Way)* to second road *(Barnfield Road)*. Turn R (N) to junction with The Ridgeway. Cross at the island into Hazelmere Road (N). Continue past entrance to junior school (L) and at school boundary turn L along alley, then bear R through wood *(Sky's Wood)* back to car park.

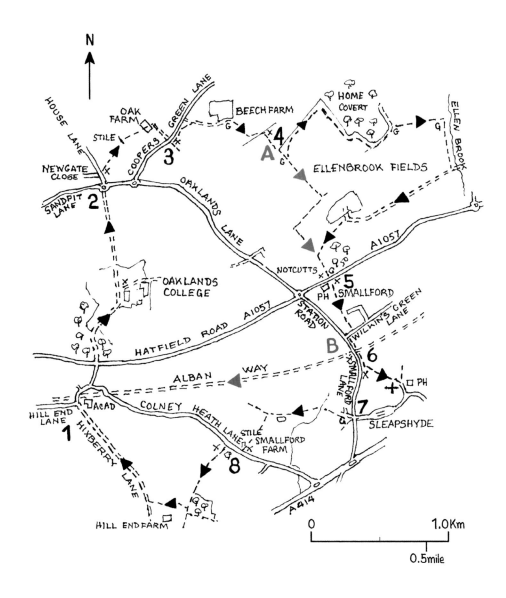

Total Distance 11.2km / 7.0 miles
Alternative A: 2.1km / 1.3 miles shorter
Alternative B: 1.8km / 1.1 miles shorter

# OAKLANDS, ELLENBROOK FIELDS, & SLEAPSHYDE

Park (a) in Hixberry Lane near junction with Hill End Lane, GR 179-069
OR   (b) at Notcutts Garden Centre & Cafe, GR 197-077.  Turn R on verge
to start of Item 5

**1** Return to Hill End Lane *(past Links Academy R)*, bear R (N), then L at roundabout into Colney Heath Lane, then turn L into Hatfield Road. Use crossing to main entrance of Oaklands College *[POI 63]*. Continue (N) along drive. The drive bears L past college buildings and roundabout R, and soon continues as a gravel track down to road *(Sandpit Lane)*.

**2** Cross road to asphalt path opposite, beside House Lane and in a few metres at junction with Newgate Close, cross House Lane to signpost opposite. Go through gap in hedge, then up field (NE) past power line post L and over the stile. Bear R towards Oak Farm and through gates between two large barns to farm road. Turn R (SE) to road *(Coopers Green Lane)*.

**3** Carefully cross road, turn L past signpost onto path with hedge L, then bear R (NE) through wood to an access road. Turn R (E) and just before gate to Beech Farm, bear R along fence with farm L. Join a track going forward then L over quarry conveyor belt. Bear R (SE) then along path to gate into Ellenbrook Fields *[POI 64 & 65]*. Alternative route A starts here.

**4** Alternative route A: *(shortens route by 2.1km / 1.3 miles, using rights of way)*. At gate into Ellenbrook Fields, continue on wide path for 400m to cross-hedge. Turn R (SW) on path with hedge L. Follow hedge for 300m, then turn L and forward to kissing gate at road *(Hatfield Road)*.

**OTHERWISE,** turn L (NE) onto path for 450m to wood *(Home Covert)*, then turn R (SE) for 350m with wood L to cross-path. Turn L then R to gravel cross-track. Turn L (NE) for 150m with trench *[POI 64]* on R to kissing gates *(the trench was dug for the film Saving Private Ryan)*. Take LH gate and bear R (E) on path with fence R for 500m through gate and cross-path. Turn R (S) with stream *(the Ellen Brook [POI 66])* L for 400m to concrete road *(old aircraft taxiway)*. Turn R (SW) for 800m to end of concrete road, then bear L on grass path for 350m. At multi-path junction, go forward through hedge to join path L (S) between hedges to kissing gate at road *(Hatfield Road)*.

**5** **(Start (b) is here)**. Carefully cross road *(noting Notcutts Garden Centre and Three Horseshoes PH R)*, past signpost onto path with field L, and past end of cul-de-sac L. This path emerges onto a lane *(Wilkins Green Lane)*, where turn R to Station Road. Turn L (S) onto asphalt path *(Peggy's Path)* sloping down to cross the Alban Way *[POI 67]*. Alternative route B starts here.

**6** Alternative route B: *(shortens route by 1.8km / 1.1 miles)*. At the Alban Way turn R (W) to lane *(Hill End Lane)*. Turn L to return to **start (a)**.

**OTHERWISE,** continue (S) along path with hedge R beside road. At next signpost bear L (SE) onto path across field. At junction of paths turn R past the Plough PH onto road in Sleapshyde. Turn R along Sleapshyde Lane to junction with road *(Smallford Lane)*.

**7** Carefully cross road to R of signpost *(RH finger says leading to footpath 11)*. Go through narrow gap with gate R onto concrete road into Smallford Pits *[POI 68]*. Bear R on track to a cross-ditch *(the Butterwick Brook)*. *(In this area, paths are denoted by green-covered concrete "cone waymarks" topped with metal posts)*. Continue across open area to pass large dew pond. Turn L (SW) along line of cone waymarks to a stile, leading to boardwalk and past Smallford Farm L to road *(Colney Heath Lane)*.

**8** Carefully cross road and turn R along pavement to end of wood and signpost *(footpath 38)*. Turn L (SW) along path, with hedge L, then through hedge past first tree. Continue with hedge R along and downhill to a path. Turn R (W) along path, leading to cross-track *(Hixberry Lane)*. Turn R along track back to **start (a)**. To return to **start (b)**, continue along Hixberry Lane to junction with Hill End Lane, then continue from Item 1.

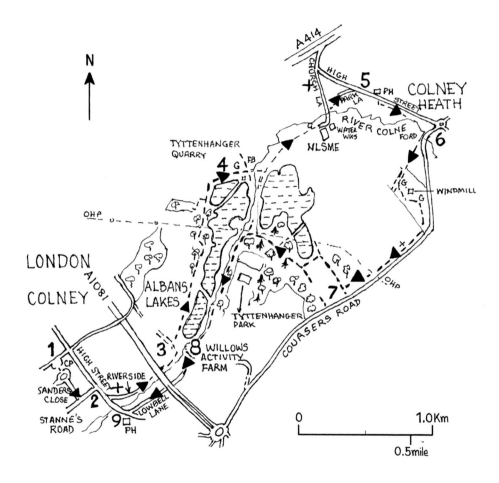

Total Distance 10.2km / 6.3 miles

# LONDON COLNEY, RIVER COLNE, & COLNEY HEATH

Park **(a)** in car park in Haseldine Road, London Colney *[POI 69]*, GR 177-041
OR **(b)** in car park by St Peter's Church *[POI 69]*, GR 182-037
OR **(c)** in public car park next to Colney Heath School, GR 201-061

**1** **(a)** At rear of car park, take asphalt path (SE) between housing. Cross circle of housing to path opposite leading to road end *(Sanders Close)*. At The Green, turn L (NE) along road *(St Anne's Road)*, then R into High Street. Go over the crossing, and continue R along road until just before the bridge. Turn L (E) into Riverside then, at signpost before entering car park, follow gravel track with St Peter's Church L.

**(b)** Track is at rear of church car park.

**(c)** Turn L onto High Street to start at Item 5.

**2** The track follows the River Colne *[POI 70]*. Cross access road leading to industrial estate. In 150m, just before reaching another road, turn R down towards the river and continue past footbridge R under the A1081. At the far side continue along river bank to and through gate into Willows Activity Farm *[POI 71]*.

**3** Cross road and turn L onto path following road bend. After a short distance as road continues L uphill, turn R along track with hedge and lakes R *[POI 72]*). Where track turns L, continue straight on, through woodland, and where path meets an access track, bear R (NE). Continue to a metal gate with Tyttenhanger Quarry works L.

**4** Cross to gap in fence, turn R then cross river. At end of fence, turn sharp L, then over quarry conveyor belt. Cross quarry access road *(view of lake and seasonal birds)* and follow path (NE) with hedge L and fence R. Go through barrier, past the Model Railway site *[POI 73]* and Water Works to road *(Park Corner)*. Go along road and cross river. Immediately turn R onto path past white City of London coal duty marker *[coal post, POI 74]* and across into lane *(Park Lane)* to road *(High Street, Colney Heath [POI 75])*.

**5** **Start (c) is here)**. Turn R (E) along road past Crooked Billet PH to village hall R. Turn R through car park with village hall L onto heath. Turn L (E) on heath to where river goes under road *(second coal post is to L near High Street)*.

**6** Turn R (S) to cross river *(using ford or road bridge)* then stay on L edge of heath. At corner of heath turn L onto farm track, then R 100m to gate on L. Go through gate, then bear R diagonally across open land *(former windmill L [POI 76] may be visible)*, through gap in hedge. Bear L to gate and road *(Coursers Road)*, then turn R between road and fence. Go through gap in hedge ahead *(noting third coal post L)* onto bridleway with road L, continuing past signpost under HV power lines and to woodland. Turn R then L through wood to concrete access road.

**7** Turn R (NW) along access road for 300m to waymark and track L. Turn L (SW) along track over quarry conveyor belt, then R (NW), with conveyor belt R. Continue on track, turning R then L to foot of HV power pylon. Turn L (S) along path for 1.0km with river bank on R *(Tyttenhanger Park and House [POI 77] are on L)*.

**8** At Willows Activity Farm L, continue (SW) using gates with river R to concrete access road. Cross, go through gate along fenced track, turn L at A1081 embankment, to lane *(Lowbell Lane)*. Turn R (SW) under A1081 with housing L and lakes and river R, to High Street opposite the Bull PH.

**9** Turn R onto High Street, cross bridge *[POI 69]* over river *(note picturesque houses on Waterside L and adjacent High Street)*. To return to **start (b)**, turn R into Riverside back to car park by church. To return to **start (a)**, continue along High Street, cross at crossing, then turn L at St Anne's Road and R at Sanders Close back to car park. To return to **start (c)**, cross bridge over river, turn R into Riverside, go through car park by church to track at rear, and continue from Item 2.

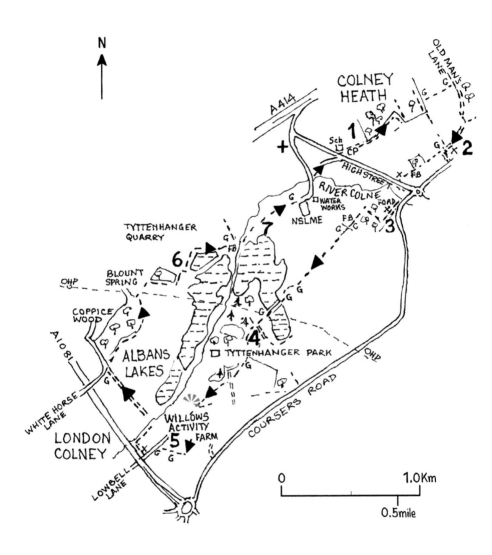

N

COLNEY HEATH

OLD MANS LANE

A414

Sch

HIGH STREET

RIVER COLNE

WATER WORKS

NSLME

FORD

FB

X FB

TYTTENHANGER QUARRY

FB

OHP

BLOUNT SPRING

COPPICE WOOD

A1081

ALBANS LAKES

TYTTENHANGER PARK

OHP

COURSERS ROAD

WHITE HORSE LANE

LONDON COLNEY

WILLOWS ACTIVITY FARM

LOWBELL LANE

1

2

3

4

5

6

7

+

0          1.0Km

0.5mile

Total Distance 9.5km / 5.9 miles

# COLNEY HEATH, OLD MAN'S LANE, & TYTTENHANGER

**Park in public car park next to Colney Heath School, GR 201-061**

**1** From far end of car park go (NE) along track with football club L. Continue on field path with woods on L and around field to cross-path. Turn R and immediately L, then continue with woods L. At next cross-path, turn L (N) on track, then shortly turn R (NE) through barrier. Continue with hedge L through next barrier and onto track. Turn R (S) for 500m along track *(known locally as Old Man's Lane)* to edge of housing and paths to R.

**2** Turn R through barrier, then L (SW) onto path beside houses *(ignore track to R)* and continue across field and footbridge. Go through barrier and continue to next barrier onto road *(High Street, ignore all side paths)*. Cross road, turn L then R *(at bus shelter)* onto heath, past white City of London coal duty marker *[coal post, POI 74]*. Continue (S) over the River Colne *[POI 70] (using ford or road bridge)*, to signpost.

**3** Stay on L edge of heath past line of trees R, then turn R (NW) into wooded border of heath. Continue for 200m to waymark and cross-path. Turn L (SW) across field, gated footbridge, and wide field. Go through hedge, then round paddock *(ignore kissing gate into paddock)*, turning R and L. At second kissing gate and waymark, turn R (SW) downhill and between lakes *[POI 72], (chance to see seasonal birds)*, then up through kissing gate. Go across cross-track, over quarry conveyor belt, and a second cross-track into woods.

**4** Go through woods, over footbridge with gate. Continue (SW) with trees R, then across field and access road with gates either side. Continue across next field to gate to R of wide farm gates *(look back to Tyttenhanger Park and House [POI 77])*, then to signpost *(footpath 004 to Lowbell Lane)*. Continue through Willows Activity Farm *[POI 71]* car park, then with fence R, to pedestrian crossing. Go over, turn L, then R after 40m, cross second car park to signpost *(footpath 4)* and kissing gate. Go through this and the next kissing gate, then cross field, and go over ditch to waymark. Turn R (W) and keep ditch to R through some kissing gates to lane *(Lowbell Lane)*.

**5** Turn L for 80m to signpost *(footpath 52)*, then R on path with A1081 embankment to L. Turn R (NE) now with river to L to gate and farm road. Turn L onto road over river, then bear L to use path to R of road. At junction of path and roads, go uphill on concrete farm road towards woods *(Coppice Wood)*. At gate, go to R side of hedge *(ignore track ahead)* to wood, turning R (NE). Follow edge of wood, eventually turning R, L & R downhill and over cross-track.

**6** Just past far end of small car park, turn L on path through wood *(ignore paths down to lake)*. When path meets access track, bear R (NE). Continue to metal gate with Tyttenhanger Quarry works L. Go forward to gap in fence, turn R then cross over river. At end of fence, turn sharp L, then forward over quarry conveyor belt and quarry access road *(view of lakes and seasonal birds)*.

**7** Continue (NE) on path with hedges L through barrier. Pass Model Railway site *[POI 73]* and Water Works onto road *(Park Corner)* and across river. Once over, turn R, passing another coal post to signpost and end of lane *(Park Lane)*. Go along lane to road *(High Street, Colney Heath [POI 75])*. Turn L back to car park *(note Crooked Billet PH to R)*.

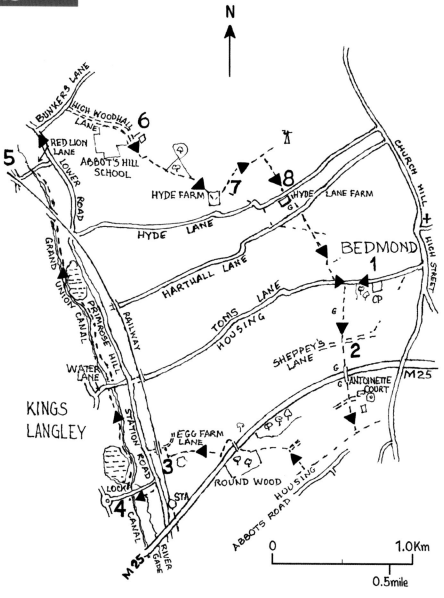

Total Distance 10.4km / 6.5 miles

# BEDMOND, GRAND UNION CANAL, & NASH MILLS

**Park in car park in Toms Lane** *(Bedmond Recreation Ground) [POI 78]*, **GR 095-035**

**1** From car park, turn L (W) for 250m down Toms Lane to path between Nos.190 and 188. Turn L (S) up steps onto path with fence R and hedge L. Go through kissing gate and down field to cross-track *(Sheppey's Lane)*.

**2** Cross track and continue (S) up path to cross gated footbridge over M25 *[POI 79]*. Continue, crossing access road *(to Antoinette Court, the former Ovaltine Dairy Farm [POI 80])* to kissing gate and cross-path. Turn R (SW) along path with housing L and field R. At next cross-path turn R (NW) to farm access lane. Bear L (W) *(passing Woodside Farm House L)*, over M25. Continue down road *(now Egg Farm Lane)* passing wind turbine and former Ovaltine Egg Farm L, carry on downhill.

**3** Follow road under railway bridge to T-junction with Station Road. Turn L (S) along this road for 300m and cross just before King's Langley Station *[POI 81]*, then turn R (W) along fenced path. Cross bridge over the River Gade *[POI 82]*, continue along boundary fence, then cross the Grand Union Canal *[POI 83]* by second bridge.

**4** Turn L down steps, then L (N) onto towpath and go under bridge. Follow towpath for 2.2km, crossing to other side of canal at first road *(Water Lane)*, and under railway bridge. 400m after the railway bridge, bear R to road *(Red Lion Lane)*, *(do not use footbridge L)*.

**5** Turn R (NE) to roundabout, then L (N) along Lower Road. At Bunkers Lane *(on R)*, carefully cross onto L pavement of Bunkers Lane, go uphill and cross to R pavement when possible. Take next turning R (SE) up High Woodhall Lane. Go past Abbot's Hill School entrance R *[POI 84]* and continue uphill along access road past tennis club R. Continue on track leading to farmhouse. Ignore signposted track L, instead bear R (SE) onto wooded path.

**6** This path continues along boundary with farmhouse L and through trees to waymark. Bear L as indicated and continue steeply downhill with hedge R. At foot of hill continue steeply uphill through wood into field. Bear R with hedge R to top of hill and Hyde Farm.

**7** At a low, wooden, finger post R, turn L (NE) *(towards Pimlico)* along track between barns. Continue on field path with hedge R leading towards radio masts. Before reaching them, turn R (SE) at waymarked gap in hedge along field path, then fenced path, into lane *(Hyde Lane)*.

**8** Turn L and in 40m R (SE) through gate past Hyde Lane Farm. This fenced path leads through gate onto lane *(Harthall Lane)*. Cross lane to gate and path (SE) towards gap in hedge. Go through gap, then keep hedge L into alley *(gardens, then houses on R)* to emerge onto road *(Toms Lane)*. Turn L for 250m back to car park.

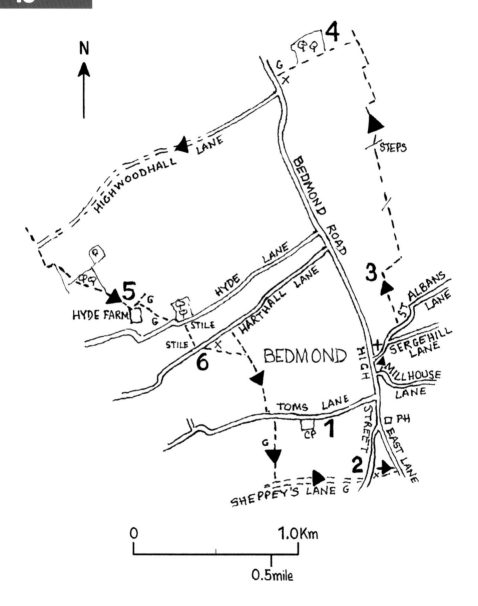

Total Distance 9.3km / 5.8 miles

# BEDMOND, WOODHALL END, & HYDE FARM

**Park in car park in Toms Lane** *(Bedmond Recreation Ground) [POI 78]*, **GR 095-035**

**1** From car park, turn L (W) for 250m down Toms Lane to path between Nos. 190 and 188. Turn L (S) up steps onto path with fence R and hedge L. Go through kissing gate and down field to cross-track *(Sheppey's Lane)*. Turn L (E) up track to gate and through barrier on L to road *(Bedmond Road)*. Turn L for 80m to signpost opposite.

**2** Carefully cross road and take path to R of metal fencing, across field to signpost and sunken asphalt track *(East Lane)*. Turn L up to road *(Bedmond Road)*. Turn R (N) past Bell PH, past roundabout to Millhouse Lane. Turn R for 40m to signpost at 'Pie Corner'. Turn L down drive, keeping L on path with garden to R, along path to Sergehill Lane. Bear R (NE) for 150m along St Albans Lane to signpost on L. Turn L (N) on path with paddocks L and then through scrub.

**3** At field turn R to end of hedge R and waymark. Turn L across field towards tree. Go through gap in hedge and continue with line of trees R. At second hedge, go up steps through gap at power line pole. Turn R then almost immediately L (N) with hedge R. At end of hedge, turn R then follow path L between fields. Keep on path, then track, with hedge L, to cross-hedge and path junction.

**4** Turn L (W) on path with hedge, then wood R, to kissing gate, signpost and road *(Bedmond Road)*. Turn L (S) on pavement until opposite Highwoodhall Lane. Carefully cross road and along lane (SW) with High Woodhall L. Continue on lane, track, and path for 1.8km to cross-track. Go across this and bear L (SE) on wooded path. This path continues along boundary with farmhouse L and through trees to waymark. Bear L as indicated and continue steeply downhill with hedge R. At foot of hill continue steeply uphill through wood into field. Bear R with hedge R to top of hill and Hyde Farm.

**5** At a low, wooden finger post R, turn L (NE) *(towards Pimlico)* on track between barns. At a farm gate after last barn, turn R through kissing gate. Bear L across field to opposite corner and through another kissing gate onto lane *(Hyde Lane)*. Turn L for 50m to signpost R, cross stile, then keep hedge L to signpost and cross second stile. Turn L onto lane *(Harthill Lane)* for 20m to signpost and through gap R.

**6** Bear L (E) down field to cross-path *(sometimes indistinct)* in middle of field, then bear R (SE) on path towards gap in hedge. Go through gap, then keep hedge L into alley *(gardens, then houses on R)* to emerge onto road *(Toms Lane)*. Turn L for 250m back to car park.

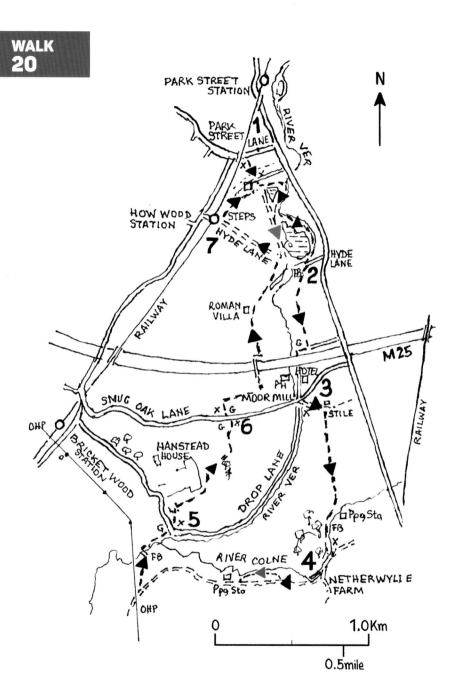

Total Distance 8.0km / 5.0 miles
Alternative : 0.3km / 0.2 mile shorter

# PARK STREET, RIVERS VER & COLNE

Park (a) in Park Street Lane, Park Street *[POI 85]*, near playing field,
GR 147-038 *(Toilets available at eastern end of playing field)*
OR (b) in Drop Lane car park, near start of Item 3, GR 151-021. Take
path to Smug Oak Lane, then turn R to track on R in Item 3
*(signposted bridleway 6)*

**1** Enter playing field at gate near pedestrian crossing and railway bridge *[POI 86]*, take asphalt path (SE) past children's play area on R. Go through gap in tree-covered embankment *[POI 87]* to road *(Branch Road)*, turn L, then R *(signposted footpath 79)*. Continue until a cross-path, then turn R. The path is between the River Ver *[POI 40]* L and lake R. Cross small footbridge, then turn L (SE) at cross-track. In 20m bear L on path with river L and lake R. Continue beside river for 500m to footbridge over river *(crossing small footbridge on the way)*.

**Alternatively:** At Branch Road go through gate; continue (SE) for 600m to footbridge over river *(shortens route by 0.3km / 0.2 mile)*.

**2** Cross car park *(accessed off Hyde Lane)*, go up steps, through gate and across open space for 500m, past an iron gate into lane *(Moor Mill Lane)*. Turn R onto track between M25 *[POI 79]* and builder's yard and continue under M25 along river bank to Moor Mill *[POI 88]*. Go around Moor Mill, following access road to road *(Smug Oak Lane)*. *(Drop Lane and its car park are to R)*.

**3** **(Start (b) is here)** Carefully cross road, then bear L on track *(signposted bridleway 6)*. In 170m with stables to L, turn R (S) and over stile. Continue on path for 500m with field edge and ditch L. At bank of the River Colne *[POI 70]* turn R for 200m towards power line and wooden footbridge. Cross and continue through wood to farm drive. Turn L, cross bridge over river, then before farm gate, take short path R (W) onto track.

**4** Pass Netherwylde Farm on R *[POI 89]*, then go 1.4km past pumping station R *[POI 90]* and several waymarked routes. **Alternatively:** take signposted path (footpath 20) at kissing gate R, re-joining route after 500m at another kissing gate. When track bears L, and HV power line pylon is visible ahead, turn sharp R onto waymarked path across *(sometimes muddy)* field. Cross footbridge, then turn R (NE) along river bank past confluence of the Rivers Ver and Colne to lane *(Drop Lane)*.

**5** Cross lane to track opposite. Go (N then NE) along track with garden wall of Hanstead House to L *[POI 91]*. Follow track (NE then N) with wall L to signpost by gate. Turn R (NE) along concrete access road, through woodland, then bear L (N) to road *(Smug Oak Lane)*.

**6** Carefully cross road and go through kissing gate opposite. Continue (N) on path for 100m, turn R (E) onto fenced path for 200m, then turn L (N) up steps, through gate and over M25. On far side turn R (E) for 20m down to waymark at gate. Turn L and continue (N) with wire fence R for 500m to information board about a Roman Villa. Bear R downhill to meeting of tracks, then turn L (W) on track *(Hyde Lane)* for 500m to steps just before gate at railway level crossing.

**7** Turn sharp R (NE) down steps onto track past school boundary on L. Turn L at cross-track, then through gate to Branch Road with school L, and continue across playing field back to Park Street Lane. To return to **start (b)** continue from Item 1.

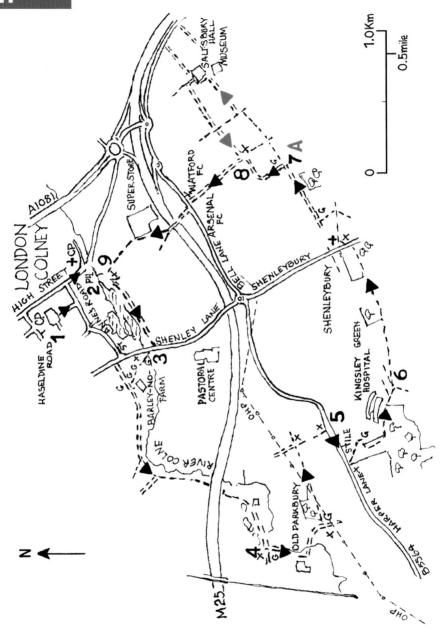

Total Distance 11.0km / 6.8 miles
Alternative: 1.7km / 1.1 miles longer

# LONDON COLNEY, OLD PARKBURY, & SHENLEYBURY

Park (a) in car park in Haseldine Road, London Colney *[POI 69]*, GR 177-041
OR   (b) in car park by St Peter's Church *[POI 69]*, GR 182-037

**1** (a) At rear of car park, take asphalt path (SE) between housing. Cross circle of housing to path opposite leading to road end *(Sanders Close)*. Where this meets The Green, turn L (NE) along St Anne's Road, then R (SE) into High Street. Bear R before the bridge and go past the Green Dragon PH R.

(b) Cross High Street to Green Dragon PH, *(it may be possible to go under the bridge)*.

**2** Turn L and cross footbridge over the River Colne *[POI 70]*. At first signpost, turn R (W) along grassy path then track over footbridge. Turn R for 700m along track with Broad Colney Lakes R *[POI 92]*, and hedge L. At a fork in the track continue (W) *(ignoring track L)* beside river. At cross-path, continue on path *(ignore footbridge R)* onto road *(Shenley Lane)* at white City of London coal duty marker *[coal post, POI 74]*.

**3** Cross road and turn R over river for 20m to signpost L. Go down steps L and through kissing gate. Bear R (NW) diagonally across field, through two kissing gates *(bear R for second)*. Keep Barley Mo Farm L, to next kissing gate and junction with farm access road. Bear L (W) on bridleway for 700m, with former Napsbury Hospital to R *[POI 93]*. Where the track turns R, bear L (S) along path with river and hedge L and go under M25 *[POI 79]*. Bear R (SW) through trees then between fences past lake R and Springfield Farm L. Continue on farm access road for 200m to signpost at cross-track.

**4** Turn L (S) on bridleway towards tall building *(with Old Parkbury to R [POI 94])*. Bear L to cross bridge over river. At cross-track, turn L (E) onto bridleway *(signposted to Harperbury)* for 700m, passing under HV power lines. At signposted cross-track, turn R (S) onto bridleway to road *(Harper Lane)*.

**5** Carefully cross road onto pavement, turn R (SW) for 300m to signpost and stile on L. Cross stile and bear L (SE) along path across field into woodland. Go through kissing gate and turn R (S) with wire fence R and former Harperbury Hospital L *[POI 95]*. Continue (S then SE) with buildings L to emerge onto access road at Margaret Cottages. Bear L (E), *(ignoring fork R)* and take clear track up a slope to lone tree, *(ahead is site of WWI RFC aerodrome [POI 96])*.

**6** At lone tree, bear R (E) on path diagonally across field to R edge of woods, then bear L (NE) inside edge of woods. At cross-track continue on path with hedge R, then fenced path to road *(B5378 Shenleybury [POI 62])*. Turn L and cross road at island. Go up steps to L into Shenleybury Churchyard, then turn R and L through churchyard to fence, keeping St Botolph's Church to L *[POI 97]*. Turn L, go around end of fence, then bear R across field to centre of small copse. Go through copse then turn L (N) onto path with hedge L. At hedge end, turn L and R to cross-track. Turn R (NE) on track between hedges for 500m, then turn L (N) by a gate.

**7** An Alternative route starts here *(extends route by 1.7km / 1.1 miles)*. At gate, continue (NE) on path then track for 800m through gate at de Havilland Aircraft Museum *[POI 98]*. Turn L then R around white house, then past Salisbury Hall *[POI 99]*. Turn L (N), go past entrance road, then turn L. Continue (SW) on tracks and paths for 700m to signposted cross-path after metal posts, then turn R.

**OTHERWISE**, follow track N, then NE, to signposted cross-path before metal posts. Turn L.

**8** Go (NW) along path between hedges *(with training grounds of Arsenal FC L and Watford FC R)*. Continue to access road and B556 *(Bell Lane)*. Use crossing to track and go over M25. Go down steps on R and bear L (NW) to boundary of Superstore R. Continue (NW) with hedge R to and through hedge gap, then past trees R to kissing gate. Go through, cross small bridge, and River Colne footbridge.

**9** Bear R to Green Dragon PH, then L up to High Street. To return to **start (b)** opposite, cross road into Riverside and back to car park by church. To return to **start (a)**, continue L along High Street, turning L at St Anne's Road, then R at Sanders Close back to car park.

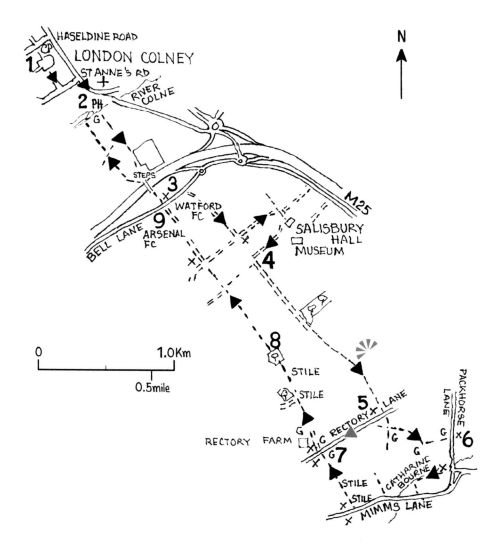

N

HASELDINE ROAD
LONDON COLNEY
ST ANNE'S RD
RIVER COLNE
2 PH
STEPS
WATFORD FC
SALISBURY HALL MUSEUM
M25
BELL LANE
ARSENAL FC
9
3
4
8
STILE
STILE
5
RECTORY LANE
PACKHORSE LANE
LANE
6
RECTORY FARM
7
STILE
CATHARINE BOURNE
STILE
STILE
MIMMS LANE

0                    1.0Km

0.5mile

Total Distance 11.2 km / 7.0 miles
Alternative: 1.4km / 0.9 mile shorter

# LONDON COLNEY, SALISBURY HALL, & MIMMS LANE

Park (a) in car park in Haseldine Road, London Colney *[POI 69]*, GR 177-041
OR (b) in car park by St Peter's Church *[POI 69]*, GR 182-037

**1** (a) At rear of car park, take asphalt path (SE) between housing. Cross circle of housing to path opposite leading to road end *(Sanders Close)*. Continue to where this meets The Green, turn L (NE) along road *(St Anne's Road)*, then R (SE) into High Street. Bear R before the bridge and go past the Green Dragon PH, R.

(b) Cross High Street to Green Dragon PH opposite, *(it may be possible to go under the bridge)*.

**2** Turn L (SE) and cross footbridge over the River Colne *[POI 70]*, then cross a brook. Continue (SE) through kissing gate with trees L to boundary fence L (SE) of Superstore. Continue R to steps up to bridge and cross over M25 *[POI 79]* onto gravel track to meet road *(Bell Lane)*. Use crossing and turn L (NE) for 100m.

**3** At the entrance to UCL and Watford FC Sports Grounds, turn R through gates and along concrete access road. Bear L across car park and past a roundabout. Bear R (SE) along concrete track passing house R, with hedge L. At cross-hedge, turn L (NE) along track, then road, for 350m. The road turns R (SE) to Salisbury Hall entrance *[POI 99]*. Turn R (SW), then L and R past the gate of de Havilland Aircraft Museum *[POI 98]*. Continue along track for 300m, then turn L (SE) at hedge.

**4** Continue uphill (SE) between fields past a wood to gap at top of the hill *(look back for view of St Albans)*. Continue down grassy path with hedge L, becoming a track between hedges. This leads to path with fence L and hedge R, emerging onto lane *(Rectory Lane)* at Foxhollows Farm.

**5** An Alternative route starts here *(shortens route by 1.4km / 0.9 mile)*. At Rectory Lane turn R (SW) for 500m along lane to Rectory Farm, then turn R at kissing gate. This rejoins the main route at Item 7.

**OTHERWISE**, turn L along lane and in a few metres turn R (S) along lane, passing Pinks Cottage R. At cross-path, under power line, turn L (E) through kissing gate and across field following power line. In L corner of field go through kissing gate. Continue with hedge L, through kissing gate and along L edge of field through next kissing gate into lane *(Packhorse Lane)*. *(Rabley Park Farm is to L)*.

**6** Turn R (S) along lane past Rabley Park L, Rabley Willow R, and over stream *(the Catharine Bourne [POI 100])*. Where lane turns L, turn R (SE) along signposted footpath 20 *(ignore signposted footpath 21)* through gate into field with hedge and stream R to field corner. At corner, turn L and R up steps, then keep fence to R. At corner, turn L (S) up onto lane *(Mimms Lane)*. Turn R (W) over stream again and past Catherine Bourne Farm R. In a further 300m is a signpost L *(footpath 18)*. In opposite hedge, cross stile (NW) into field with row of trees R. Cross another stile to kissing gate and cross lane *(Rectory Lane)*.

**7** Go (NW) through kissing gate opposite into field, then through another kissing gate onto farm track with fences on each side. Go downhill passing gates on each side to gate and stile R near small plantation. Cross stile, bear R diagonally past trees to fence and row of trees R. Cross stile in cross-hedge, go across small field and into wood *(seasonal bluebells)*. At far side, emerge onto farmland.

**8** Look (NW) *(towards Superstore)* for gap in hedge in the distance. Head towards this across the field, passing a grass airstrip R and hollow L *[POI 101]*, then through the gap. Cross playing field and continue through another gap, then along path between hedges *(with training grounds of Arsenal FC L and Watford FC R)* leading to access road and B556 *(Bell Lane)* again.

**9** Use crossing to track opposite and go over M25. On the other side, ignore steps R and continue along track *(Blind Lane)* with hedge L. Ignore all paths L and R until cross-track *(signposted Watery Lane)* by the River Colne. Turn R (NE) onto track, then after 10m turn L to cross small footbridge. Continue to original path and over river. Bear R to Green Dragon PH, then L up to High Street. To return to **start (b)** opposite, cross road into Riverside and back to car park by church. To return to **start (a)**, continue L along High Street, turning L at St Anne's Road, then R at Sanders Close back to car park.

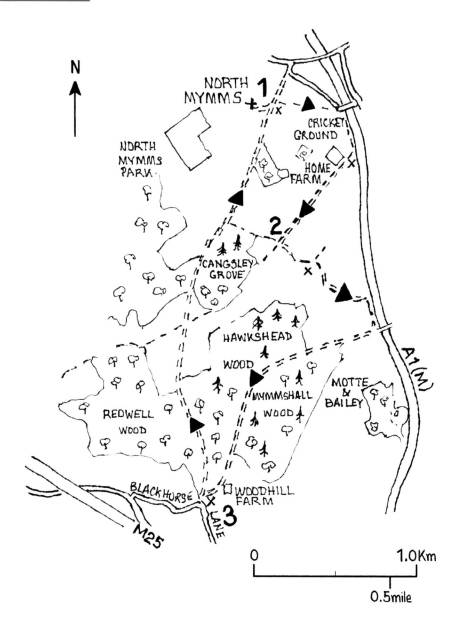

N

NORTH MYMMS **1**

NORTH MYMMS PARK

CRICKET GROUND

HOME FARM

**2**

CANGSLEY GROVE

HAWKSHEAD WOOD

MYMMSHALL WOOD

REDWELL WOOD

MOTTE & BAILEY

A1(M)

BLACKHORSE
WOODHILL FARM

LANE **3**

M25

0        1.0Km

0.5mile

Total Distance 6.6km / 4.1 miles

# NORTH MYMMS, & REDWELL WOOD

**Park near St Mary's Church *[POI 102]*, North Mymms, GR 222-045**

**1** From the church *(North Mymms House [POI **103**] may be visible to SW)* return to the approach road, turn R  then L (SE) through kissing gate onto path across field.  Pass cricket field R *(ignoring kissing gates into and out of it)*, to and through third kissing gate.  Go up steps, over track and down to lane.  Turn R under A1(M) *[POI **104**]* footbridge.  At signpost *(byway 05)* continue beside A1(M) to junction with bridleway on R.  Turn R (SW) onto concrete track for 750m to cross-track.

**2** Turn L (SE) on track between hedges.  Ignore signposted track L *(byway 5)*, take track uphill, keeping hedge L then follow wooden fence to footbridge at A1(M).  Do not cross footbridge, but keep on track with hedge L, ascending into woods.  After the top of the rise keep to the wider track through the woods, ignoring all minor paths.  The track descends through woods to track with lane *(Blackhorse Lane)* L and signpost ahead.

**3** Turn R (N) through gates around house onto bridleway.  Continue up and down hills for 2.5km *(ignoring all side paths and tracks)* to road, church, and back to start, *(near the end, North Mymms House may be visible to L)*.

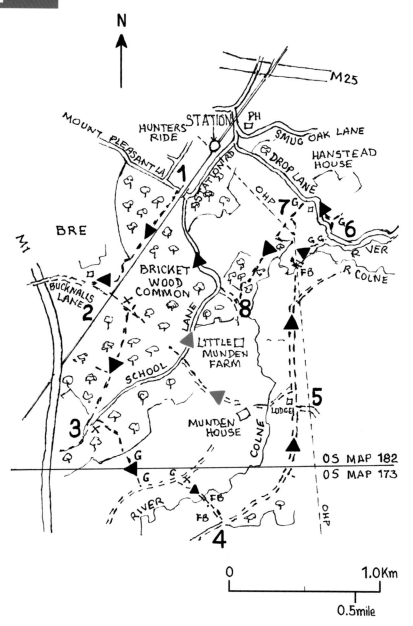

N

M25

HUNTERS STATION PH
RIDE
MOUNT PLEASANT LA
SMUG OAK LANE
HANSTEAD
HOUSE
STATION RD
DROP LANE
OHP
7 G
1
G
6
BRE
M1
G.G
R VER
BUCKNALLS
LANE
BRICKET
WOOD
COMMON
FB
R COLNE
2
LANE
8
SCHOOL
LITTLE
MUNDEN
FARM
3
MUNDEN
HOUSE
LODGE
5
COLNE
G
OS MAP 182
G
OS MAP 173
RIVER
FB
OHP
FB
4

0                                    1.0 Km

0.5 mile

Total Distance 8.6km / 5.3 miles
Alternative: 2.5km / 1.5 miles shorter

# BRICKET WOOD, & COLNE VALLEY

Park **(a)** along Hunters Ride (or side roads), Bricket Wood *[POI 105]*,
 GR 131-018,
OR **(b)** Start from Bricket Wood Railway Station *[POI 86]*, GR 135-020

NOTE: OS Explorer Map No.173 also covers part of this route

**1** **(a)** From Hunter's Ride, turn L into Mount Pleasant Lane. Just before railway bridge, cross road onto bridleway opposite into woods.

**(b)** From the station, turn R (SE) onto road *(Station Road)* and along pavement for 450m to junction with Mount Pleasant Lane and School Lane. Turn R under railway bridge, then cross road onto bridleway opposite into woods.

Continue with railway boundary fence L, passing cross-path and continue with fences L and R. The path bears R (W) onto asphalt road *(Bucknalls Lane), (to the R is the Building Research Establishment [POI **106**])*.

**2** At house *(Far End)*, turn sharp L (SE) onto path *(signposted Herts Way)*. Enter wood, cross railway footbridge and continue to signpost for footpath 48. Turn R (S) and continue *(ignore all cross-paths)* past the "Fox With His Teeth Drawn" *[POI **107**]* to lane. Turn R to street sign *(School Lane)* with path opposite *(just beyond is the former Old Fox PH)*.

**3** Turn L (SE) onto path through woods to path between fields leading to drive to Munden House *[POI **108**]*. Turn L (NE) to gate and cattle grid, then turn R (SE) across field to footbridge over the River Colne *[POI **70**]*. Cross field and another footbridge to junction of tracks.

**4** Turn L (NE then N) *(Munden House may be visible across valley on L)*, passing track on R to reach River Lodge.

**5** An Alternative route starts here **(shortens route by 2.5km / 1.5 miles)**. At River Lodge turn L (W) along farm track and bridleway. Cross footbridge and continue (W then NW) on bridleway to lane *(School Lane)*, with Munden House L. Turn R along lane and continue to junction with Mount Pleasant Lane. Here turn L to **start (a)**, or R to return to the station, **start (b)**.

**OTHERWISE**, bear R (N), and continue under HV power lines. When bridleway bears R (NE), turn onto path across field towards steel footbridge. Cross over the river, then turn R along river bank *(note confluence of Rivers Ver [POI **40**] and Colne)*. Continue to road *(Drop Lane)*.

**6** Cross to bridleway opposite, going (N) for 100m *(Hanstead House is ahead [POI **91**])*, then turn sharp L onto narrow path with gate at far end and back into Drop Lane. Turn R, and after a L and R bend, turn L at kissing gate.

**7** The path goes L (SW) of a barn and continues with hedge on L. Cross field and under HV power lines to woodland opposite. Continue (SW) with wood L, then where wood turns R, take narrow path through wood then down to gate in boundary fence. Cross field and plank bridge onto driveway for Little Munden Farm.

**8** Turn R (NW) along driveway *(a public footpath)*. At junction with lane *(School Lane)*, turn R (NW). This pleasant wooded lane leads to junction with Mount Pleasant Lane and Station Road. Here turn L back to **start (a)**, or R back to the station, **start (b)**.

# POINTS OF INTEREST

| POI | DESCRIPTION | WALK |
|-----|-------------|------|

**01  WHEATHAMPSTEAD** - From Wathemstede. Given to Westminster Abbey **1, 2**
by Edward the Confessor c960. See also POIs **14** & **34**.                   **7**
Information boards, plaques and leaflets give more information.

**02  ST HELEN'S CHURCH** - The church is built of Totternhoe stone and faced **1, 6**
with flint. The nave and chancel are of near equal length with a dominating
late C13 crossing tower, from the floor of which the bells are rung. In the
church is an early C14 octagonal font and many monuments, including
a brass to the parents of Abbot John of Wheathampstead of c1436, an
alabaster tomb chest of Sir John Brocket and his wife of 1558, many Garrard
tablets and the Garrard memorial of c1630. There is a small bronze statue
of Apsley Cherry-Garrard, the Antarctic explorer [POI **15**], who is buried in
the graveyard.

**03  DISMANTLED RAILWAY** - The Hertford, Luton & Dunstable Railway opened **1, 6**
the line in 1860. It was taken over by LNER and closed to passengers in
1965. **Keeper's Cottage** is the old level crossing keeper's house. See also
POI **16**.

**04  RIVER LEA** - From Lug meaning 'bright water' rises from a natural spring **1, 2**
in the chalk at Leagrave, N of Luton, to join the Thames at Limehouse. It is **6, 7**
not classified as a chalk stream.
At one time the river was the boundary between the Danes (S) and Saxons
(N).

**05  BATFORD** - During WWII, a large prisoner of war camp was located W of **1**
Common Lane. It is now housing.

**06  KATHERINE WARINGTON SCHOOL** - Katherine Warington (1897-1993) **1**
lived locally and worked at Rothamsted [POI **27**]. She is known for her
research into the beneficial impact of boron and boric acid on plant and
bean fertility.

**07  MACKERYE END** - Grade I listed, symmetrical brick front of 1665 with **1**
Dutch gables with pedimented tops and elaborate chimney stacks. As a
child Charles Lamb (1775-1834), essayist and critic, visited his great-aunt,
Anne Gladman, who lived here.
In an older building on the site, John of Wheathampstead, Abbot of St
Albans (1420-1440) was born.

**08  TURNERSHALL FARM** - Two significant burial sites on a C2 Romano **1**
British estate were discovered in 2002. Excavations revealed finds of late
Iron Age and Roman occupation.

**09  GUSTARD WOOD COMMON** - From Goshamstedwoode of c1272 taking **1**
its name from the Old English name of 'gorse or juniper'. The Common is
designated a County Wildlife Site.
A 9-hole golf course was created in 1892, extended to 18 holes in 1923.
The club's first professional, Horace Rawlins, won the inaugural US Open
Championship in 1895.

| POI | DESCRIPTION | WALK |
|---|---|---|

**10  GUSTARD WOOD COTTAGES** - Include five listed buildings. Nos.17, 10 and 8/9 are C17/C18 (8/9 has C18 front). No.6 is a row of four late C18 cottages. Rustling End is a row of three buildings of similar age.  **1**

**11  THE MANOR OF HERONS** - Family name of Heron or Hayron c1201. In 1695 Edward Strong, quarry owner and mason, employed 65 masons on the building of St Paul's Cathedral. With his fortune he bought estates in Hertfordshire, including Herons in 1716. He lived in St Albans and was buried at St Peter's.  **1**

**12  BURY FARM COTTAGES** - A long timber-framed and jettied building of C15/C16, whose use has changed much since it was connected with Wheathampsteadbury Manor.  **1**

**13  CRINKLE-CRANKLE WALL** - These walls undulate in a series of curves so a thin wall can stand without buttressing. This rare Victorian example is the only publicly accessible one in Hertfordshire. On both E & W sides, there is an entrance to the garden that is being restored with a petanque court, seating and sensory garden.  **1**

**14  WHEATHAMPSTEAD** - The best group of buildings includes **The Miller & Carter Steak House (The Bull).** The **C16 Mill** and beyond the river, and **Wheathampstead Place**, originally a medieval hall house. A Tudor archway fronts the garden. See also POIs **01** & **34**.
Before the roundabout, up steps R, is the restored **Railway Station** [POI **03**].  **1, 2 6, 7**

**15  LAMER PARK ESTATE** - A manor house was rebuilt by William Garrard in c1555. The house was replaced during the Georgian period and the park remodelled by Nathaniel Richmond and after his death by Humphrey Repton. In 1892 the estate was inherited by Apsley Cherry-Garrard [POI **2**]. As a member of Captain Scott's expedition to Antarctica, he was one of those who found their last camp. The house was demolished in 1949.  **2**

**16  AYOT GREENWAY** - Trail extending from Wheathampstead to Ayot St Peter along the line of the dismantled railway [POI **03**].  **2**

**17  REDBOURN** - Redbourn derives its name from 'reedy stream'. Over the centuries there have been over 20 spellings of the name.
Watling Street, the Roman road, ran through what is now the High Street. In the coaching period (c1760-1840) when it was the London to Holyhead main road, there were 19 inns listed in the High Street.
The main industry in the village was straw plaiting and in 1851 there were over 400 people involved in the industry.  **3, 4 8, 11**

| POI | DESCRIPTION | WALK |
|-----|-------------|------|

**18 REDBOURN COMMON** - From ancient times the area (formerly known as The Heath) gave villagers Common Rights that were protected by the Abbot of St Albans.
Ownership passed through several hands before ending up with the Gorhambury Estate. The 4th Earl of Verulam handed over the Common to the Parish Council in 1947.
Although it is possible cricket was played here in 1666, the **Cricket Club** was established in 1823. In the early C20 there was a 9-hole golf course here.
Close by is the **former school** and next to the **Cricketers PH** is **Redbourn Museum** in a house built for the manager of Woollams Silk Mill that was on the site until 1938. During WWII, Brooke Bond moved from London to the site. The mill site was developed for housing in the 1990's.
**3, 4 8, 11**

**19 CHURCH END** - The site of the early village. There are 12 listed buildings in the street, including the former **Work House** (late C18) and the timber framed **Hollybush PH**.
**3, 11**

**20 ST MARY'S CHURCH** - With Norman tower & nave. The chancel is early C14, the S aisle mid C14 and the porch mid C15. Roman brick was used in the tower and at the E end, chalk and flint. Inside there is a fine C15 rood screen.
**3, 11**

**21 M1 MOTORWAY** - The first long distance motorway in Britain consisting of three lanes. The first phase was opened in 1959.
**3, 4 11**

**22 THE AUBREYS** - From Auld Burth - 'Old Fort'. An Iron Age fort c250BC extending to c22 acres surmounted by a double bank and ditch.
**3**

**23 REVEL END** - The farms of Little and Great Revel End have houses and barns from the C17. An earlier name was Rutherfield Farm, after Adam de Rutherfield of 1307.
**Note:** There are many timber framed farm houses in the area named after Redbourn residents, including Hogg End (John Hogg 1307), Butlers (John Botiler 1455), Dane End (Roger de Dane 1294) and Old Jeromes (The Precentor of the Abbey of St Alban held land, 'Jerommes' 1455).
**3**

**24 HERTFORDSHIRE SHOW GROUND** - Hertfordshire Agricultural Society was founded in 1801 and there is reference to ploughing matches at Hatfield in 1879. The current County Showground was established in Redbourn in 1962.
**4**

**25 HARPENDEN** – From Herpedene (1060). Until 1859, Harpenden was in the Parish of Wheathampstead, with St Nicholas Church as a Chapel of Ease. From 1880's it developed as a commuter town.
**5, 9**

**26 HARPENDEN COMMON** - Was part of the medieval Manor of Rothamsted. In 1901, the western parts were made over to the Harpenden UDC by Sir Charles Lawes [POI **27** & **28**]. The remaining Manorial Rights were purchased in 1935.
**Harpenden Races** - Occasional horse races were held before regular racing commenced in 1848, when about 10,000 people attended the first meeting. The course started from near the present golf club to go S over the fields of the **Childwickbury Estate** [POIs **52** & **53**]. The last race was held in 1914.
**5, 9**

**27  ROTHAMSTED RESEARCH** - The world's first agricultural research station. **5, 9**
It is considered to have been founded in 1843 by John Bennet Lawes [POI
**26** & **28**] on the appointment of Joseph Henry Gilbert. They collaborated
in the development of experiments on plant nutrition. Lawes concerned
himself with the value of bones as a fertiliser, which led him to produce
the first commercial fertilisers from mined calcium phosphate, the profits
of which he spent on experiments for enriching the soil. Many of these
experiments continue to this day (now known as the Classical Experiments)
and are still providing valuable data. In 1889, Lawes founded the Lawes
Agricultural Trust with an endowment of £100,000 to ensure the continuance
of agricultural research. The Trust now owns the Rothamsted Estate.

**28  ROTHAMSTED MANOR HOUSE** - A large imposing red brick mansion       **5**
built mainly 1630-1650, incorporating an earlier medieval dwelling. The
S front has mullion and transom window casements, a three-storey porch
with Gothic cupola and Dutch gables. The great drawing room was added
by John Bennet Lawes in 1863 for his son's coming of age ball. [POIs **26**
& **27**].
It is now an events venue.

**29  NICKEY LINE** - Originally a railway opened in 1877 by the Midland   **5, 8**
Railway (later LMS), running from Harpenden, through Redbourn to Hemel   **11**
Hempstead. Passenger services were withdrawn in 1947 due to post-war
coal shortages. The track was gradually removed, with the section from
Claygate to Harpenden being re-opened in 1969 by the Hemelite Concrete
Company for transport of building blocks. The line finally closed in 1979
and the track lifted in 1982.
The course of most of the railway has been redeveloped as an 8-mile cycle
and walking route by St Albans District Council and Dacorum Borough
Council. It was opened in 1985 as the Nickey Line.

**30  PIMLICO PLACE** - Terrace of 16 red and blue brick cottages were built in   **5, 9**
1822 by the Benefit & Annuitant Society of St Albans. It seems probable
that the cottages were built as an investment to be let to farm labourers.

**31  FLOWTON PRIORY** - Early C16 timber framed building moved from   **5, 9**
Ipswich in 1925.

**32  NOMANSLAND COMMON** - Was the disputed lands of the Abbeys of St   **6, 10**
Alban to the S and Westminster to the N until it was agreed in 1429 that the
grazing rights should be shared. The heathland to the N of Ferrers Lane is
some of the best in S Herts, supporting a wealth of wildlife and rare plants.
In the Second Battle of St Albans on 17 February 1461, the Yorkist army
fled to the Common.
The area was notorious for highwaymen and in 1652, 18 year old Katherine
Ferrers attacked a wagon from which shots were fired. She fled on
horseback to her home, Markyate Cell, where she was found dead by
servants. **Ferrers Lane** and the **Wicked Lady PH** are named after her.
Cricket has been played here since 1826 and the first horse race organised
by Thomas Coleman took place in 1830. Prize fights were held mid-century
and cock fighting continued illegally into the C20.

**33 CROSS FARM HOUSE & BARNS** - There is a glimpse from the gateway of the C15 or early C16 Grade II* hall house with C17 two storey porch. — 6

**34 WHEATHAMPSTEAD** – See also POIs **01** & **14**. — 6
**The Swan PH** was built in c1500 as an open hall, the frontage was added in c1750. On **Brewhouse Hill** the **former school** of 1869 is of flint with brick in zig-zag bands with grey & green slate roof. **The Old Brew House** operated from 1781-1904.

**35 DEVIL'S DYKE** - An earthwork of pre-Roman age. It is c460m long with a maximum depth of 13m. It formed part of the Belgic settlement, which may have been the capital of Cassivellaunus before his defeat by the Romans. — 7

**36 JOHN BUNYAN PH** - The PH (the Prince of Wales until the 1950's) recalls the author of The Pilgrim's Progress who is said to have frequently lodged and preached in the cottage opposite, of which only the chimney stack remains. — 7, 10

**37 FLINT BRIDGE & FISHING ALCOVE** - A folly on the Brocket Estate [POI **48**] over the River Lea [POI **04**]. — 7

**38 WATEREND HOUSE** - The Grade II* listed house was built c1610 to the N of the ford. The W front with three gables and two-storey bay windows has fine chimney stacks. Originally a manor house of the Jennings family and possibly the birth place of Sarah Jennings (1660-1744), later Duchess of Marlborough. — 7, 8
Waterend Barn was moved to St Albans in 1938.

**39 CUMBERLAND HOUSE** - A Grade II* listed, seven-bay, house once owned by the Duke of Cumberland (victorious at Culloden 1746), who used it as a hunting lodge. — 8

**40 RIVER VER** - This chalk stream begins at Lynch Lodge, Kensworth and joins the River Colne [POI **70**] S of St Albans. Flow is restricted due to water extraction. — 8, 20 24

**41 HARPENDEN GOLF CLUB** - Founded in 1894. Moved to its present site (18-hole) in 1930. — 8, 9

**42 HAMMONDS END HOUSE** - The path rises 30m to the Grade II*, three-storey, five bay, dark red brick house of early C18 seen above the hedges. — 8, 9

**43 REDBOURNBURY** - Grade II* listed. Originally a manor house belonging to the Abbey of St Alban. It incorporates a large C15 hall. — 8

**44 REDBOURNBURY WATERMILL** - Grade II* listed, mid C18 and later. The mill mechanism was repaired after a disastrous fire in 1987. — 8

**45 DOLITTLE MILL** - Previously known as Bettespool. A new mill was built c1706 and soon after was converted to paper making. After a fire in 1783, it reverted to grinding corn until milling ceased in 1928. — 8

**46 RIVER RED** - A small tributary of the River Ver. Rising on Redbourn West Common [POI **18**] and joining the River Ver [POI **40**] W of The Chequers PH. — 8

**47**  **THE OLD HOUSE** - C16 timber framed building originally The Bull Inn   **5, 9**
(1586), the oldest inn in Harpenden. Occupied as a house since the 1860's.

**48**  **BROCKET HALL** – A Grade I square red brick mansion by James Paine,   **10**
built for Sir Matthew Lamb, later Lord Melbourne and completed in 1780.
His son, William, married Caroline Ponsonby, whose sensational behaviour
and her infatuation with Lord Byron, he had to contend with. After her
death, William became Prime Minister (Lord Melbourne, 1834, 1835-41).
On his death it passed to his sister, who married Lord Palmerston, (Prime
Minister 1855-58 and 1858-65). It was also a favourite country retreat of
Queen Victoria.
The house is now a conference centre with two golf courses.

**49**  **PUDDING STONE** - This small piece of stone (see also section on **Geology**)   **10**
was erected in 1429 to mark the boundary between Wheathampstead and
Sandridge. It was moved from the cricket outfield in 2014 and set within a
semi-circular seat.

**50**  **BUNCEFIELD** - Beyond the M1 [POI **21**] is the Buncefield Oil Storage   **11**
Depot linked by pipeline to refineries at Ellesmere Port & Shell Haven. On
11 December 2005 explosions (measuring 2.4 on the Richter Scale) caused
a major fire.

**51**  **BATCHWOOD HALL** - Lord Grimthorpe (1816-1905) designed and built   **12**
the house that was altered in 1912. He designed the clock mechanism that
chimes Big Ben. At his own expense, he designed and built the W front at
the Abbey of St Alban.
The house is now a night club with an adjacent sports centre and golf club.

**52**  **CHILDWICK BURY HOUSE** - The mansion has been much altered, firstly   **12**
by ship owner Henry Toulmin in 1854 and later by Sir John Maple of Maples
Stores in c1900. He bred and raced horses and built up the Childwick
Stud into the largest horse-breeding establishment in Britain. Jack Barnato
Joel, a diamond and gold merchant, bought the estate in 1907 and he and
his son, 'Jim', were amongst the most successful British owner/breeders
for almost all of the C20. The house was bought in 1978 by film director
Stanley Kubrick (1928-99). See also POIs **26** and **53**.

**53**  **CHILDWICK GREEN** - **St Mary's Church** (1867) and adjoining school were   **12**
designed by Sir George Gilbert Scott. On the green is a late C19 winding
gear for a well. The imposing **Lodge**, with its Scottish baronial style turret
and wrought iron gates, was built in 1897 and has elaborately detailed red
brick and terracotta decoration. See also POIs **26** and **52**.

**54**  **SANDRIDGE** – The 1086 Domesday Book refers to Sandruage held by the   **13, 14**
Abbot of St Albans.
The High Street contains a number of listed buildings, including the timber
framed C16 **Rose & Crown PH**, **Darby's Stores** and **The Heartwood Tea
Rooms**. Also, in the High Street is the **Green Man PH** and nearby the re-
cased C16/C17 **Queen's Head PH** beside **St Leonard's Church** [POI **58**].

| POI | DESCRIPTION | WALK |
|-----|-------------|------|

**55  HEARTWOOD FOREST** – In 2009, the Woodland Trust acquired the 858- **13, 14** acre site, which included some ancient woodland. Since then over 600,000 trees have been planted.
The **Community Orchard** - 600 fruit trees, including apples, pears and plums have been planted since 2011.
The **Arboretum** - Contains all 60 trees and shrubs native to the British Isles.

**56  MIDLAND MAIN LINE RAILWAY** - The Midland Counties Railway (later **13** LMS) built the track to Bedford in 1852, with a link via Hitchin into Kings Cross.  The section from Bedford to St Pancras was not completed until 1868.

**57  POUND FARM** - The track passes between the C15/C16 house, that has **13** been altered, and barns of the same period.

**58  ST LEONARD'S CHURCH** - From the W can be seen the flint faced tower **13, 14** and front of 1866-67.  Inside, the Roman bricks in the chancel and arch suggest they were part of the church consecrated by Bishop Losinga of Norwich (1094-1119).  In the late C14, the chancel was rebuilt and the rood screen erected retaining the Roman Arch.  On its E side are charming figures on sloping ledges.

**59  MARSHALSWICK** - From John & William Marschal, who held it for the **14** Abbey of St Alban 1271-1377.  After 1921 the estate was split up and developed for housing.

**60  JERSEY FARM WOODLAND PARK** - Evans Farm was renamed **Jersey** **14** **Farm** in the 1960's.  Planning permission was granted to build on 118 acres of farmland and building work started in 1977. 55 acres of park were saved from development and in 1991, the first phase of planting was carried out. Information boards and leaflets give more information.
At the entrance is a memorial to the Royal Navy Association and other service units.

**61  WIRELESS STATION** - In 1939 the site was a wireless intercept station for **14** the Foreign Office used to intercept traffic between enemy governments and their embassies.  Later, Germany used high-speed encryption and transmission equipment (Enigma machines). Their messages were recorded here and sent to Bletchley Park for decoding.
In 1973 the site was handed over to the Home Office and is now run by the Defence Science & Technology Laboratory.

**62  SHENLEY / SHENLEYBURY** - From Scenlai (1086) – 'bright or beautiful **14, 21** woodland glade'.  See also POIs **96** & **97.**

**63  OAKLANDS** - Conversion of a Georgian house with a castellated tower **15** built for William Knight.  The park of 335 acres was bought by Hertfordshire County Council in 1920 for training agricultural students.
Oaklands College is now a general Further Education College.

| POI | DESCRIPTION | WALK |
|-----|-------------|------|

**64** **HATFIELD AERODROME** - Developed by the de Havilland Aircraft   **15**
Company in 1930, and a factory built in 1934. In WWII, the Mosquito, which
was developed at Salisbury Hall [POIs **98** & **99**] was built here. A hard
runway was laid in 1947 and the military Vampire and commercial Comet
aircraft were developed and built here. Hawker Siddeley acquired de
Havilland in 1960 and further mergers took place until British Aerospace
was formed in 1978. The last aircraft to be built here was the HS146
commercial airliner, which first flew in 1981, with production ending in 1993.
The facilities closed in 1994.
After its closure the site was used by Steven Spielberg to film 'Saving
Private Ryan' and 'Band of Brothers'.
The site has subsequently been developed for gravel extraction, housing,
the University of Hertfordshire campus and a nature park [POI **65**]

**65** **ELLENBROOK FIELDS** - This 400 acre site was originally farmland before   **15**
becoming part of Hatfield Aerodrome [POI **64**]. Welwyn Hatfield Borough
Council announced its opening as a nature park in 2010.

**66** **ELLEN BROOK** - A tributary of the River Colne [POI **70**]. Rising in Hatfield   **15**
and joining the River Colne W of Colney Heath.

**67** **ALBAN WAY** - Originally the railway line between St Albans Abbey Station   **15**
and Hatfield developed by the Great Northern Railway (later LNER) in 1865.
It closed to passengers in 1951 and to freight in 1969.
The route was sold to St Albans District Council and Welwyn & Hatfield
Council in 1982 and developed as the 6.5 mile Alban Way, a walking and
cycling route.

**68** **SMALLFORD PITS** - Old gravel workings, now a local wildlife site. The lake   **15**
is managed for fishing by Verulam Angling Club.

**69** **LONDON COLNEY** – From Colnea (1209-1235) meaning 'island by the   **16, 21**
River Colne'. The village was on the coaching route from London to   **22**
Holyhead and later the A6 passed through the village until the bypass was
built in 1959.
The **Telford Bridge** was built in c1775 before being improved by Thomas
Telford (1757-1834) as part of his work on the London to Holyhead road
between 1823 & 26. To the W of the bridge is the ford.
**St Peter's Church** is a Norman revival style church built by George Smith
in 1825.

**70** **RIVER COLNE** - This chalk stream rises from a spring in North Mymms   **16, 17**
Park to join the River Thames at Staines.   **20, 21**
  **22, 24**

**71** **WILLOWS ACTIVITY FARM** - Children's activity farm offering animals,   **16, 17**
shows, play area, tractor rides, etc.

**72** **ALBANS LAKES** - Is part of a 180 acre estate and consists of several lakes   **16, 17**
created as a result of gravel extraction and a stretch of the River Colne [POI
**70**] used for angling.

**73** **NORTH LONDON SOCIETY OF MODEL ENGINEERS** - Founded in 1944.   **16, 17**
The site has a boating lake, model railway and space for traction engines.
Open on some Sundays between May and October.

**74**  **CITY OF LONDON COAL DUTY MARKERS** (also known as 'city posts'  **16, 17**
and 'coal posts') - Erected in 1861 to mark the point at which duty became  **21**
payable on coal entering London.  The tax was introduced in 1667 to
increase revenues to pay for redevelopment of London following the plague
and the Great Fire of London.  It was repealed in 1889.
There are two posts in London Colney and four in Colney Heath.

**75**  **COLNEY HEATH** - Originally c200 acres and known as Tyttenhanger Heath,  **16, 17**
owned by the Manor of Tyttenhanger, an early C12 manor given to the
Abbey of St Alban, whose Abbot used it as a country retreat.  It is said that
Henry VIII and Thomas Wolsey stayed here during the plague.  Tyttenhanger
is the site of a lost medieval village, where 321 people died of the plague.

**76**  **COLNEY HEATH WINDMILL** - The four-storey tower windmill was built  **16**
in the 1850's.  The sails were removed in 1890, when it was converted to
steam power and closed in 1906.  It is now residential accommodation.

**77**  **TYTTENHANGER HOUSE** - Grade I listed red brick country mansion built  **16, 17**
in 1655 probably by Peter Mills (1598-1670).  Later alterations were carried
out.  On the front ridge is a large wooden clock turret surmounted by an
octagonal bell chamber and cupola.  It is now a conference centre.

**78**  **BEDMOND** - The birthplace of Nicholas Breakspear, later Pope Adrian IV  **18, 19**
{1154-59), the only Englishman to be Pope, who is believed to have been
born c1100 at Breakspear Farm in the village.
The **Church of the Ascension** is a rare surviving example of a 'tin
tabernacle', a pre-fabricated church made from corrugated galvanised iron.
It was built in 1880 at a cost of £80.

**79**  **M25 MOTORWAY** - The M25 or London Orbital Motorway is a 117-mile  **18, 20**
motorway that encircles almost all of Greater London.  Opened by Margaret  **21, 22**
Thatcher on 29 October 1986, with a ceremony between Junctions 22 & 23.

**80**  **OVALTINE FARMS** - Ovaltine, of Swiss origin, came to the UK in the  **18**
early C20 when a factory was built by the canal at Kings Langley.  After
production began in 1913, Albert Wander, son of the founder, bought two
farms of c450 acres.  The Dairy Farm was rebuilt to imitate that built for
Queen Mary Antoinette at Versailles.  By mid C20 close to 1,500 people
were employed at the factory, but production ceased in 2002.  The Dairy
Farm was converted to residential use (Antoinette Court) and the Egg Farm
to offices for a renewable energy company, with a wind turbine on site.  The
art deco style Ovaltine factory in Kings Langley has become a well-known
local landmark and has now been redeveloped as luxury apartments.

**81**  **WEST COAST MAIN LINE RAILWAY** - The first railway to have a service  **18**
into Hertfordshire was the London & Birmingham Railway (later LMS)
opened in 1838 into London Euston Station.

**82**  **RIVER GADE** - A chalk stream which runs from the Chilterns at Dagnall to  **18**
Rickmansworth, where it joins the River Colne [POI **70**].

**83** **THE GRAND UNION CANAL** - Originally known as the Grand Junction Canal, it was built 1793-1805 affording a link between the industrial Midlands and the Thames before railways were built. From the 1960's it has been mainly used by pleasure boats.  **18**

**84** **NASH MILLS** - By 1768 the cornmill had been altered to make paper. John Dickinson purchased it in 1811 as an addition to his nearby Apsley Mill and the company developed into one of the world's largest stationary businesses in the C19 & C20. Dickinson originally lived in the mill house, called Nash House. In 1836 he built a new home, Abbot's Hill, which was sold in 1912 to be developed into **Abbot's Hill School**.  **18**

**85** **PARK STREET** - Settlements existed in the Mesolithic Period and later clearings and track ways were created in the forest. The Romans built Watling Street; later Saxons, Danes and Normans controlled the area, but did not settle. The Abbots of St Albans owned much of the area and the main activity was farming until the Victorians developed the railways and improved the roads.  **20**

**86** **ABBEY FLYER RAILWAY** - The line was opened by the London & North Western Railway in 1858 from Watford Junction and was the first railway to reach St Albans at the Abbey Station.  **20, 24**

**87** **DISMANTLED RAILWAY** - The Midland Railway (later LMS), Park Street Branch was opened in 1868 to join their main line at Napsbury Junction. It was closed in 1910.  **20**

**88** **MOOR MILL** - Mentioned in the Domesday Book, Moremyll was owned by the Abbey of St Alban. From c1400, the miller was asked to pay rent in the form of eels, caught in the waters around the mill, for the Abbey's refectory. Behind the current brick faced mill house is the C19 mill, with central hoist doors and two-storey hoisting bay. In the PH / restaurant, the mill wheel can be viewed through a glass panel.  **20**

**89** **NETHERWYLDE FARM** - On crossing the river there is a view of the river and the red brick bridge. From the central drive can be seen the late C18 brick front, with flint porch of the house that was originally a two-bay hall house that is surrounded by timber barns and brick out-buildings.  **20**

**90** **PUMPING STATIONS** - A number of ground water pumping stations exist along the Colne valley, which have been built to resemble barns at the request of the Yule family, who owned the land. [POI **91**].  **20**

**91** **HANSTEAD HOUSE** - The house was built for the Yule family in 1925 on a 1200-acre site. After Sir David Yule [POI **90**] died, his widow and daughter bred Arabian horses. In 1957 the American evangelist, Herbert Armstrong, bought the site for his Ambassador College that remained until 1974. It was subsequently used as a training college by CEGB and HSBC until 2011, after which the site was bought for development.  **20, 24**

**92** **BROAD COLNEY LAKES** – A nature reserve with three lakes, created as a result of gravel extraction in the 1920's.  **21**

| POI | DESCRIPTION | WALK |
|---|---|---|

**93**   **NAPSBURY HOSPITAL** - Formally the Middlesex County Asylum opened in 1905. Louis Wain (1866-1939), famous for his cat paintings, was a patient. In WWI it was a military hospital. It closed in 1998 and the site developed for housing.   **21**

**94**   **OLD PARKBURY** - The site has been occupied since Neolithic times and cremated remains of c4000BC have been excavated. Early Saxon sunken floor huts and evidence of Medieval Parkbury have been found. Sir Francis Walsingham (1532-1590), principal secretary to Elizabeth I and popularly known as her spymaster, lived here in the former manor house. The C15-16 farmhouse has now fallen into disrepair.   **21**

**95**   **KINGSLEY GREEN HOSPITAL** - On 25 October 1925, the Hangars Certified Institute was opened, so named because of the three remaining hangars on the site [POI **96**]. In 1934, the Middlesex Colony for the mentally handicapped was opened; it later became **Harperbury Hospital**. Much of the site closed in 2001 and part of it has been redeveloped as Kingsley Green Hospital.   **21**

**96**   **LONDON COLNEY AERODROME WWI** - The aerodrome at Shenleybury began as a Royal Flying Corps safe landing ground in early 1916. In July 1918 it became officially known as No.41 T.D.S. (Training Depot Station). It closed in 1919.
**Harperbury Hospital** was then developed on the site [POI **95**].   **21**

**97**   **ST BOTOLPH'S** - The church is now a house. Nicholas Hawksmore (1661-1736), who assisted Sir Christopher Wren and Sir John Vanbrugh and built several London churches, was buried here. There is a distinctive monument to the Muller family. William Muller's daughters, Eva and Henrietta, were prominent members of the women's suffrage movement. Eva is one of those mentioned on the statue to Millicent Fawcett in Parliament Square. In the churchyard a giant yew tree has a girth of 5m suggesting it is 600-700 years old. The water tower of the former Shenley Hospital stands prominently on the ridge [POI **62**].   **21**

**98**   **DE HAVILLAND AIRCRAFT MUSEUM** - The first aviation museum in Britain when it opened to the public on 15 May 1959. Contains a collection of military and commercial aircraft manufactured by de Havilland Aircraft Company [POI **64**].   **21, 22**

**99**   **SALISBURY HALL** - The Grade I brick house surrounded by a moat is a fragment of the original built by Sir John Cuttes, Treasurer to Henry VIII and modernised in c1670. Nell Gwynne lived in a small lodge when she visited with Charles II. Former residents include Lady Randolph Churchill and Sir Nigel Gresley, the locomotive engineer.
It became the design centre for the de Havilland Aircraft Company and where the famous WWII Mosquito was designed [POIs **64** & **98**]. It returned to residential use in 1959.   **21, 22**

**100**   **CATHARINE BOURNE** - Tributary of the Mimmshall Brook and River Colne [POI **70**]. Rising in Shenley [POI **62**] and joining the Mimmshall Brook at South Mimms.   **22**

**101**   **AIRSTRIP** - Home of The Hertfordshire Microlite Club.   **22**

**102** **ST MARY'S CHURCH** - Parish church of North Mymms for over 700 years. Inside is a rare Elizabethan pulpit and monuments by sculptors. Peter Scheemakers and John Bacon Snr. — **23**

**103** **NORTH MYMMS HOUSE** - This Grade I listed late Elizabethan house was built in c1600 by Sir Ralph Coningsby. The N front is of two storeys with gabled wings and a central porch. Having passed through many owners as a private house, it was occupied by Glaxo 1992-2018. The property is now used for conferences and a wedding venue. — **23**
The River Colne [POI **70**] starts from a spring in the park.
On 19 September 1784, Vincent Lunardi flew in a balloon from the grounds of The Honourable Artillery Company just to the N of the City of London. He had with him a pigeon, a cat and a dog. The pigeon flew away, then as the cat was cold, he came down at North Mymms, where he handed the cat to a woman before continuing his flight to Standon.

**104** **A1(M) MOTORWAY** - Motorway section of the A1 between South Mimms and Stevenage. The section around Hatfield was completed in 1986. — **23**

**105** **BRICKET WOOD** - From Bruteyt (1228) – 'a bright, colourful, small island on a piece of marsh land'. — **24**
Bricket Wood Common - This poor agricultural land was used for common grazing by the residents of the hamlets of Old Bricket Wood and Smug Oak. It is now an area of diverse habitats of ancient woodland, hornbeam coppice, wet lowlands heath / acid grassland, ponds and seasonal streams, supporting a wide range of flora and fauna.

**106** **BUILDING RESEARCH ESTABLISHMENT** - Established in 1921 and as a world leading, multi-disciplinary, building science centre. — **24**

**107** **THE OLD FOX WITH HIS TEETH DRAWN** - Is a thatched house with dormers within a picturesque setting behind a pond. Formally a PH (The Fox then The Old Fox), it was bought in 1893 by teetotaller Arthur Holland-Hibbert (later 3rd Viscount Knutsford), who revoked the licence in c1917 due to the abuse of drinking by the newly attracted in-comers. It became a Temperance House serving teas, sweets and flowers under its current name. It is now a private house. — **24**

**108** **MUNDEN HOUSE** - A largely Victorian Country House. The house is used extensively for filming, as it is close to Elstree Studios. — **24**

# GENERAL LOCAL INTEREST

*Descriptions in this preface and in the Points of Interest [POI]*
*relate to the areas visited on the walks*

## GEOLOGY & LANDSCAPE

**Bedrock Geology:** The area is underlain by a thick succession of chalk of Upper Cretaceous Age (100 – 83 million years old). Chalk is a fine-grained limestone with bands of Flint nodules. Although the chalk is generally not far below the surface, exposures as at Redbournbury Quarry are uncommon. Aquifers within the chalk are the main water supply for the region.

Much of the overlying geology has been eroded and there are only a few outliers of the Eocene Reading Beds (56-55 million years old). They are relatively thin and consist of sands and clays which have been used for brick making in the past. Hertfordshire Pudding Stone (consisting of rounded flint pebbles in a very hard siliceous cement) is also of this age and specimens can be seen displayed throughout the county.

**Superficial Geology:** To the N and W of St Albans, the chalk is covered by a thin layer of clays with large amounts of broken flint in them.

To the S and E of St Albans, the superficial deposits are mainly outwash sands and gravels from glaciers and development of the large Thames river system during the Ice Age. These are locally quarried for sand and gravel.

**Landscape:** St Albans sits in the Vale of St Albans, a low flat lying area between the hills around Redbourn and Harpenden and the South Hertfordshire Plateau towards Shenley and Radlett. The Vale of St Albans was the course of the proto-River Thames prior to the Ice-Age. During the Ice-Age the river gradually moved southwards into its present course.

Dry valleys, which are typical of chalk landscapes, are common features in the N and W of the area.

## LOCAL LAND USE

**Agriculture:** The majority of non-urban land is classified as 'good to moderate' and is ideal for growing cereals and rape. It is also suitable for grasses for harvesting and grazing through much of the year. Dairy farming no longer holds the position it once held and now considerable amounts of grazing land are used for horses.

**Woodland:** Ancient woodland, of which there has been a decline in the C20, is dominated by hornbeam that was traditionally coppiced. The remaining woodland is secondary (naturally established since 1600) or new plantations in open ground.

**Heathland and Acid Grassland:** Most such land survived the C18 enclosures as common land. There was a slow decline until c1940, since when conifers, gravel extraction and conversion to recreational use have had an impact. Most importantly, the change of management practices has resulted in scrub and woodland growth, which has dramatically reduced these habitats.

# LOCAL BUILDING MATERIALS

**Stone:** The two principal building stones are chalk and flint. Chalk, much of which came from Totternhoe (Bedfordshire), has been used sparingly as it weathers badly. Flint is almost indestructible, but it has mainly been used for utility.

**Timber:** In the Middle Ages most cottages and barns were timber framed and its use extended into the Tudor and Stuart periods; suburban developments obliterated most of these. Many were later masked by Georgian brick and in the C20 plaster was removed to expose timbers to a state never intended by their builders. Few thatched roofs remain, as straw of a suitable length is no longer a product of wheat production.

**Brick:** The most important building materials have been brick and tile due to the excellence of local clays. The Romans made bricks that later builders re-used. By Tudor times, brick was the chosen material for those who could afford it. It was later introduced to humble timber framed building for chimney stacks.

# LOCAL PLACE NAME ELEMENTS

There are many common elements in place names including:

**Bourn / Bourne:** Stream or brook

**Bury:** Manor

**Hyde / Hide:** Saxon / Early Norman measure of land, the amount to support one family

**Stead / Hamstead:** The buildings that make up a farm ('Hamstead' is the homestead)

**Wick:** Dairy farm or trading settlement

**End:** Forest or woodland clearing, beyond the main settlement. Names including End and Green are often preceded by names of founding families.

# REFERENCES

1. **'24 FOOTPATH WALKS IN HERTFORDSHIRE'**
   St Albans & District Footpaths Society

2. **'THE HERTFORDSHIRE WAY'** - Bert Richardson, Castlemead - 2017

3. **'AN HISTORICAL ATLAS OF HERTFORDSHIRE'** - David Short (Editor),
   University of Hertfordshire Press - 2011

4. **'BRITISH LISTED BUILDINGS'**
   https://britishlistedbuildings.co.uk/england/hertfordshire

5. **ARCHITECTURAL GUIDES: The Buildings of England (Pevsner):**
   HERTFORDSHIRE - 2019

6. **'HERTFORDSHIRE GEOLOGY AND LANDSCAPE'** - John Catt (editor).
   Hertfordshire Natural History Society - 2010

7. St Albans & District Footpaths Society:    www.stalbansfootpaths.org

8. Ramblers Association:    www.ramblers.org.uk

9. Heartwood Forest:    www.heartwood.woodlandtrust.org.uk

10. Ver Valley Society    www.riverver.co.uk